Cherishing and Challenging Your Children

Cherish the children.

Love,

Jody

♡

Prov. 22:6

Cherishing & Challenging YOUR CHILDREN

JODY CAPEHART

VICTOR BOOKS®

A DIVISION OF SCRIPTURE PRESS PUBLICATIONS INC.
USA CANADA ENGLAND

Unless otherwise noted, Scripture quotations in this book are from the *New American Standard Bible,* © the Lockman Foundation 1960, 1962, 1963, 1968, 1971, 1972, 1973, 1975, 1977. Quotations marked NIV are taken from the *Holy Bible, New International Version,* © 1973, 1978, 1984, International Bible Society. Used by permission of Zondervan Bible Publishers.

Library of Congress Cataloging-in-Publication Data

Capehart, Jody.
  Cherishing and challenging your children / Jody Capehart.
    p.   cm.
  ISBN 0-89693-899-9
  1. Parenting—United States. 2. Parent and child—United States. 3. Child rearing—United States. 4. Parenting—Religious aspects—Christianity.
  I. Title.
HQ755.8.C36   1991
649'.1–dc20   91-7210
                                                                  CIP

    3 4 5 6 7 8 9 10 Printing/Year 95 94

Contents

Acknowledgments

The hearts and prayers of many very special people have enabled me to write this book. Without their prayers and encouragement, this book would be only a dream.

I want to thank my parents Chet and Donna Kvanli who are a source of constant love and encouragement to me.

I want to thank my prayer partner, Sue Bohlin, who faithfully prayed me through the good times and the tough times.

I want to thank my friend Jeri Fowler who guided and prayed me through this project, even before it went to a publisher.

I want to thank my wonderful typist Donna Trapp who patiently turned my rough drafts into ordered manuscripts.

I want to thank Scripture Press/Victor Books for giving me the idea for this book and then the opportunity to write what I feel in my heart. Thank you also, for providing a wonderful editor in Afton Rorvik who could climb inside my heart and mind and help me communicate more concisely.

Last, but certainly not least, I want to thank the hundreds of precious children who have blessed me beyond measure. I cherish you and I thank you for challenging me.

Dedication

This book is dedicated to my husband, Paul, who faithfully encouraged me to write and then helped provide "gifts of time" so I could write. This book is also dedicated to my children who bless me beyond what words could ever express. I pray every day to be the mother you need who will cherish and challenge you to be all you can be for Jesus Christ. I love each of you!

ONE

God's Unique Design

Not too long ago, when I was speaking in Denver, I had the opportunity to see a Colorado snowstorm firsthand. As I do so often, I found myself in awe of our Creator. He could have easily made each snowflake the same. But He chose to make each one completely unique. What is His purpose? I believe it is to show us how much value He places upon the uniqueness of each of His creations. God delights in individuality. Why then do we try to get everyone to conform to one set way of doing things, to produce the "canned green beans mentality"? Instead, we should strive for and rejoice with the "garden variety" that I believe our Heavenly Father created us to be.

♥ Cherishing and Challenging

We can more effectively *cherish* our children when we embrace their differences as God-given and we can *challenge* them more effectively when we learn the best ways to work with these differences. Since God has chosen us to parent this precious child, then He must be delighted to show us His way to wisely handle this unique "gift." We must have an open, teachable spirit and be willing to be humbled, lest we tumble.

We are able to cherish our children more when we can embrace these differences and acknowledge our Creator's sovereign purpose in making our child the way He did. That's easy to say when you have an easy child. It's much more difficult to say when God presents you with a difficult child. My friends had a sweet, easy-going little girl. Parenting was a joy. Then God chose to give Mike and Ann an autistic child. This godly family is a precious part of our church and school. It is such an encouraging testimony to see the positive ways they nurture and cherish Sam, just as they do their easy child, Rose. Recently they were interviewed by a major news station in our area which produced a three-part series about their family and the challenge of raising an autistic child.

As the cameras followed, Ann chased Sam around (a never-ending task). Ann said, "Control was always important to me. God chose to give me a situation completely out of my control. He cares more for our *character* than He does what we can and cannot do." In the perspective of eternity, God does care more for our character and the spiritual character we are daily working to build within our child than He does about any set of worldly standards of success.

❤ Accepting Our Children

It is often difficult to accept others, especially our own children, as the unique creations that God intended them to be. We want to force *our* way on our children and then wonder why we experience road blocks in our relationship. I believe that the reason God often gives us a mate who is much different from the way we are, is because He wants us to learn to accept differences with love and respect instead of resentment. When we try to "fix" our children's differences, they get the message "I'm not OK. Something must be wrong with me." When a child is under age five, he thinks his parents can do or say nothing wrong. So if the parent sends the message that the child is inadequate, this goes right to the core of the child and dramatically affects his self-esteem.

(More on this in the chapter on Self-esteem.) It is ironic that often the very child we seek to love and raise to be the best adult possible is the very one we hinder because we aren't sensitive to the fact that he functions differently than we do.

Let me share from my own personal experience. I am aware that I have two different sides to my personality. Part of me is outgoing and loves people and activity. The other part of me is very quiet and reflective and needs lots of alone time to be able to go back and love the people and activity again. If I don't get alone time I feel like a porcupine with its quills out to protect itself and I find myself inwardly screaming *Leave me alone!*

I have to come to peace with these two aspects of my being. For years I was afraid that I had a personality malfunction, but now I realize that both sides are equally important to who I am. I need both in order to function.

My son Christopher is very much like my quiet side. We can be quiet together for untold hours without tiring of each other. We read, reflect, talk, and love silence as well. Since most people do not see that side of me, they don't realize it's there. I am closely bonded to Christopher. I am very protective of his need for lots of alone time each day. I understand him. It is very easy to give him what he needs in that area because I understand him.

My daughter Angela is like what most people see to be the "real me." She loves activity, the more the better. She loves people and is a very social creature. With a fever of 103° she mutters, "I think I can go to church, Mom. I need to see my friends." When we spend time together, we do activity-oriented things, such as making bread, playing the piano, singing, and running errands. And we are both happy.

I experience and share my quiet side with Christopher, and I share my active side with Angela. I feel equally bonded to both children. I do not try to "fix" them because I understand them.

When we received custody of my husband's son, it was a rude awakening to have a child in the house with whom I did not feel bonded. He was very different from me. I didn't want him to see his stepmother close to two children and not to him. This grieved my spirit. I tried everything to find some way to bond with him. Since he was no longer young, he was set in his ways and it was a challenge. Finally, we found it when we began to set up "dates" to go to Christian concerts. It was at a Sandi Patti concert that Damon accepted Christ as his Savior. Now we have a bond for eternity. As I prayed about this, the Lord began showing me more ways that we can bond, and now I feel very close to him.

❤ *God's Infinite Designs*

There are so many ways that we can observe God's infinite design. As we study patterns of child development and temperaments, we can better parent our children. There are volumes written today on the various labels for these individual differences and characteristics. It can be overwhelming so I have selected just a few of these areas for us to look at. Our purpose in viewing these differences is to help us more effectively *cherish* the way God made our children and then to provide practical ways to *challenge* them to be all that God intended.

❤ *Child Development*

A child begins his individualized climb through a series of steps we call *child development.* The process is very rapid at the beginning and changes weekly. That is part of the marvel of parenting. As the child gets older, the changes are more gradual.

I was well versed in child development before my own children came along. I resolved that I would not be another one of those parents who went "nuts" (and became obnoxious) over each thing my child did and said. I would not state zealously, as many parents do, "My child really is a genius."

Well, when my children arrived, I threw the textbooks

aside and stood in awe of how truly amazing the whole process was. In fact my child WAS a genius, or so it seemed to me.

There is simply no way to prepare a parent for that amazing experience of seeing your own child become a person. Only God could have created such a profoundly intricate process. Most children go through certain predictable steps and yet each child has his/her own biological clock of development.

Child development guidelines should certainly not replace the clocks and calendars in your home, but they are a helpful tool to know what to look for. Of course, there is always the inherent danger of putting all your parental expectations in this "time schedule" basket and then being devastated if your child is not exactly where the books say he should be. There is also the prideful side of each of us that thinks our child's IQ score is directly related to the exact moment that he first sat up or took his first steps, not to mention the degree of super parenting on our behalf! It takes a wise parent to allow each child to unfold in God's perfect timing.

To parents who are lamenting over how late their child is walking, talking, or being potty-trained, I say, "Look at a group of high schoolers and tell me which one sat up first, walked first, or got potty-trained first." Obviously, it is impossible to tell. Do you know why? Because it doesn't matter! Try to tell that to a group of first-time moms comparing notes at the local park, or to the parent of a firstborn who hasn't rolled over at the prescribed time when "all the other babies in the neighborhood did."

With these warnings firmly in mind, it is wise to be familiar with several books on child development. Dr. Louise Bates Ames has written a wonderful series of books that talk about *Your One Year Old, Your Two Year Old,* etc. (Gesell Institute of Child Development). These books are profoundly interesting when you have a child that age and terribly boring when your child is past that age. This is true for the same reason that discussing the color of your child's stools is the most interesting topic when your child is a newborn and certainly the most nauseating when you do not have a child at that stage. To sum up, we must remember that child development guidelines are simply that—guidelines.

❤ Temperaments

I believe that God imprints each of us with a pattern especially designed for His purpose. One of these patterns can be identified as temperaments. I believe that we each have a strong, dominant temperament and a weaker, secondary one. I also believe that when we are reborn into God's family, we will become a more balanced blend of the four temperaments, as part of the sanctification process.

We do not study the temperaments just so we can say, "Well, that's just the way I am. I'll never change. That's the way God made me." We are to give our temperament strengths back to God to be used for His service. Likewise, we are to come to Him with our weaknesses and on our knees and *in* our weakness, He is made strong. By His grace, He overcomes or even works through our weaknesses. Thus, through the special temperament God gave us, we bring honor and glory back to God.

We must remember, however, that we tend to see life through the grid of our individual temperament. We assume that we are "right" because this is how God made us. Hence, everyone else should function this way too.

❤ Choleric Children

Choleric children want CONTROL at any cost! It is incredulous to them that Mom or Dad is in charge. They assume they should be; therefore, parents of these children are locked into a battle of wills from the very beginning. Dr. James Dobson calls this the "strong-willed child." With many of these children "iron-willed" is more like it! The secret of handling these children is to use the magic words, *"You're in charge of...."* It's amazing how well this works. Let them be in charge of things *you* want them to be in charge of like setting the table, taking out the trash, choosing their own clothes to wear, arranging their room, etc. If you don't allow this, they will simply try to take over on their own.

These children, when properly trained, will probably grow up to be great leaders, pastors, and presidents of companies. They will probably do great things for the Lord. The challenge lies in getting them raised and teaching them to be obedient. When they feel they have control over at least some things in their lives, the times when the parent must be in charge will be easier.

Our daughter is a blend of the sanguine and choleric. As a young child, she manifested more of the choleric but as she grew older, she became more of the sanguine.

Our choleric daughter was also a colicky baby. (No, the two do not necessarily go together, although I have said on occasion that a choleric child can give a parent colic!) She was a tough baby. I was convinced she was allergic to sleep. During her infancy we moved our home, moved the school, and opened a second school. That was the year that nearly did me in. To rest after the three moves, we took our eight-month-old daughter to meet my family in Minnesota. We were getting gas in Kansas, and I was rearranging things in the front seat while my husband pumped the gas. She managed to get out of her car seat and while trying to "escape," landed on her head. I picked up a bloody baby, and we rushed to the hospital. We had her in three hospitals during our one-week vacation. This was "Life with Angela."

As a school principal, I kept my children in my office until they were school age. Angela was in her little baby seat, and I was typing. Suddenly her face lit up, our eyes met, and she smiled with sheer joy. I was so happy and thought, "Finally we are bonded in love. She realizes that I'm her mother and that I love her and. . . . " None of that fluff for my daughter. She had figured out how to pull herself up and walk. There was sheer joy in her eyes as she communicated via her body language, "Bye, Mom, I'm out of here."

So much for tenderness. Her next smile came when I found her standing in her crib. You guessed it. She walked at eight months, handed me her diapers at twenty months saying she didn't want them, they were for babies, and potty trained herself. I told her she was violating all the principles I "preached" on about not rushing children. For Angela, I had to can the child development books.

💜 *Sanguine Children*

These children are sunshine. They simply want to have fun and to love and be loved. They tell you how wonderful you are. They hug you and bring you presents. They are, however, forgetful, talkative, and impulsive. They have never met a stranger and are at home in any group. They love people and interacting with them. They want approval from you so much. They may compromise on what they believe just to get approval from someone they look up to. With these children you have to train in strength of character.

The sanguine child's criteria for measuring the validity of an experience is by the degree of *fun* provided.

"How was Sunday School today?"

"Great—we had so much *fun!*"

"What was the lesson about?"

"Huh? Ahhh. I think I forgot."

"Did you remember your Bible?"

"Hmmmmm . . . no, I think I forgot it."

"Do you remember where?"

"Ummm . . . I think it was in the bathroom when I was talking to Jenny. Mom, we have this great thing planned for next Friday night. It will be so *fun!* I am going to wear my. . . . "

"Honey, did you get permission to go?"

"Ummm . . . I forgot. Sorry, Mom. But, Mom, please, can I go? It will be so *fun.*"

That's the same child, my daughter, who at age three always wanted a playmate over. She was so fun oriented that chores were always secondary. She's the child whose idea of cleaning her room is to throw everything under the bed or in a closet so no one will see it. Cleaning is definitely not fun and therefore not a valid experience.

I once found my sanguine daughter's room all "cleaned" into her buggy and covered with a blanket. It was the stench in the room that gave me a clue that all was not well in "Fun City." As I pulled out a wet (well, it was wet when she first "cleaned") swimsuit, clothes from the daily "Let's change our clothes twenty times a day parade," and peanut butter sandwiches ("Yeah, Mom, I forgot about the rule of no food in my room . . . sorry."), I now clearly saw how the "Queen of Fun" had miraculously cleaned her room in one minute.

As I dragged her in from her current "fun" to teach her some profound, life-changing lessons from this disaster, she seemed unimpressed by the depths of my dismay. She looked me straight in the eye and said, "So, hire a maid."

I will confess "visions of child abuse danced in my head," but since I teach (and "preach") that parents need to remain calm and composed under such situations I answered, "We can't afford a maid and where did you hear of this?"

"On TV." (Another reason to ship the thing to a needy family in Siberia.)

So as a dedicated discipliner, I ended her "fun" for the day and left her to "properly" clean her bedroom.

Up to age two I saw the choleric aspect of Angela's temperament. Now she is more of a sanguine—fun, loving, and eager to please. Her choleric will is still there, but it can be challenged. I am curious as to which temperament will be most evident when she is a teenager!

♥ Melancholy Children

These children are determined to "do it right." They are born perfectionists. If a first attempt isn't perfect, they may give up in total discouragement. They are serious, genius prone, artistic, moody, and deep thinkers. Childhood isn't their happiest hour. They will be happier as adults. Play doesn't mean as much to them as to the sanguine child. You have to help them accept themselves and the world as it is and love them unconditionally. They need to lighten up and be more positive. Great things may come from these children, but it is usually with a great deal of internal struggle and pain.

Our melancholy child was described by the nursery worker as "fascinating," by his teachers as "unusual," and by his family as just plain "weird." Damon definitely marched to a different drummer, but search as we did, we never found that drummer. I can write this now, for at age seventeen he has the amazing ability to laugh at himself. That's God's grace so we too can laugh. But there were times we weren't sure if we should laugh or cry.

For example, the drummer that Damon marched to was not in any of the time zones we recognize on Planet Earth. "Earth to Damon" was the most frequently used phrase in communicating to Damon. Thirty times of repeating that with increasing volume eventually granted you a "Huh?" You had to catch his eyes and put your face in his to say what you needed before he retreated into the other zone from whichever planet. He never played with toys or other children. His idea of a "good time" at age six was to have you give him a fraction, and he would tell you the decimal equivalent.

Damon was seven when Christopher was born. One day as I cooked dinner at home, I had Damon watch Christopher on the floor. The den and kitchen are joined, and I watched with delight as Damon showed him the planets and explained how many light years away each planet was. That's Damon — always willing to pass along the practical information every three-week-old baby needs in order to develop properly.

Damon could not dress himself in under one hour until after age twelve. We had to check every five minutes or he would fade into the ozone again. Directions had to be very clear. For example, one day he came down dressed for church in only thirty minutes. "Damon, we are so proud of you. But darling, why do you look so lumpy? Honey, you have your pajamas on under your clothes." His response was "Huh?"

(Looking down) "But you only said to get dressed."

All school tests showed a genius level IQ but a low functioning. Teachers would throw up their hands in dismay as to what to do with him. We often found toothpaste in the refrigerator and the butter in the bathroom. Where oh where is that drummer so we can fix him?

Please know that Damon's behavior is not all typical of a melancholy. It was difficult to determine what temperament tendency he had because he marched to another drummer. The first clue I had was the meticulous way he organized his Legos. His giftedness was a second clue. The third clue came when I saw the way he embraced research papers. He manifested what I call the "melancholy freeze." A melancholy can see the perfectly completed product in his mind but doubts his ability to produce it as perfectly as he pictures it. So the result is often a "freezing," in other words, a temporary paralysis of action.

It often takes a tremendous amount of encouraging and coaxing to get a melancholy started on a project. Have faith, his brilliant mind will take over once the inertia is overcome. Watching Damon perform in the orchestra or band now is incredible. He is completely focused and a joy to behold.

❤ Phlegmatic Children

These children are a joy because they are so easy going. They make most parents look good because they don't act up much. They are quiet, easy to please, easy to get along with, and patient. They can be stubborn and may be lazy. Properly guided, they can be one of the best servants in God's kingdom because they are peacemakers. They don't get bent out of shape over most of the things that children with other temperaments do.

My entire life I wanted a baby. As a child, I always slept with a pillow under my pjs so I would "feel" like I was pregnant. When I finally was pregnant, at age thirty, I was obnoxious. On one hand I was praising God and on the other hand, I thought I had invented the process myself. I was so happy!

Since I was already a school principal, people watched closely to see if I could live what I had been counseling parents for years. I didn't know about temperaments at that time. When Christopher was born, he looked up, coughed, and never cried. He was a calm, obedient toddler. I would say softly, "We don't touch that," and he would never go near it again. (Unlike my choleric child who took that kind of statement as an open invitation to do it again!)

Christopher made me look good! People thought my ideas of speaking softly and firmly really worked. Wiser, more experienced parents would smile and say, "Wait until you have your next child." Meanwhile, I frolicked in the false security of thinking I was Mother of the Year. The truth is that Christopher is my "Phlegmatic Phil."

Phlegmatics are wonderfully easy-going. They are compliant and very witty. My father, husband, oldest brother, and son are phlegmatics. They bless my life immensely.

I am happy that the Lord gave me children who exhibit all four temperaments. I have learned so much from their differences. As in everything, there are no simplistic answers. Children are a *blend* of these temperaments. If you want a more in-depth study of these, you should read some of Florence Littauer's books or Dr. Tim or Beverly LaHaye's books. These are listed in the bibliography.

❤ The Day of Reckoning

The day of reckoning seems to come when your precious little lamb starts school. Since you already know your child is a genius, you are not that worried. You look forward to the rest of the world acknowledging this obvious fact. Then comes the first note home with the unbelievable words that MUST have been intended for some OTHER parent: *We are having trouble with little Johnny. Can you come in for a conference?* Immediately, all of your mother-bear or father-bear instincts come out, and you are ready to do battle with this silly human being called a "teacher."

I have found after twenty years of counseling parents that NO parent is ready to deal with problems in a child. If a parent has trouble at home and the school also has trouble, the pain can be too much. If a parent has honestly not experienced the problem at home and has not the foggiest notion of what the school is talking about, the result can still be the same: DENIAL. One response is honest, the other is learned.

I always advise teachers to begin a conference by stating the positive qualities of this precious child — and EVERY child does have his positives. All of us that belong to the species called "parents" need to be dealt with gently when it comes to our own child. And yes, we ALL have our blind spots. So, if you are called in for a conference, PRAY and ask the Lord to give you eyes to see your child as he is. The more realistic we can all be, the sooner we can solve these problems. Now what are some of the problems? We will discuss a common problem that I see so often in school and church. Your child's temperament obviously affects the way he or she approaches learning, but another factor is equally important. A CHILD SHOULD BE TAUGHT IN THE WAY HE OR SHE LEARNS BEST. This is what we will examine in Chapter 2.

♥ Parent Participation

1. Am I responding age-appropriately to my child?
2. In what ways is my child like me?
3. In what ways is my child different from me?
4. How do I embrace these differences?
5. Have I bonded to my child via our similarities? Or through any differences?
6. What can I do to strengthen that bond?
7. What unique pattern do I see in each of my children?
8. What am I doing to CHERISH this uniqueness?
9. What am I doing to CHALLENGE each child to be the best he can be?
10. What am I praying for each child in terms of God's purpose for his unique pattern?

How Children Learn

Observe a young child for a few minutes and watch how he takes in information. He makes a grab for an item and immediately takes it to his mouth. As he gets older, he smells it instead of putting it in his mouth. He combines all of his five senses to truly get an understanding of what this object is all about. In this experience he begins the lifelong process of organizing and classifying information coming in via his five senses.

♥ Learning Modalities

Learning modalities is a term used to define the PROCESS through which a child learns. A modality is a sensory unit that enables us to take in information. All children are multi-sensory learners. They learn best when they can see something, hear it, touch it, and with little ones, taste it, and sometimes smell it. The three main modalities for school-age children are:

1. Visual modality: see it
2. Auditory modality: hear it
3. Kinesthetic modality: touch it

Children learn through their senses on their own during the preschool years. Any time that you as a parent want to help that learning process, here is an easy three-step plan which achieves good results:

1. *Isolate* what the child is to learn.
2. *Classify* each step of the process.
3. *Refine* the learning process.

For example, let's say you want to teach colors to a child. First, you isolate exactly what it is you want to teach. You lay out three colors. (I use tablets of colored papers or paint chips.) Then you classify the colors. "This is red. This is yellow. This is blue." Then you ask the child, "Show me red. Show me yellow. Show me blue." Then you ask the child to name the colors for you. If he can, then you can continue on to step #3. If he can't, then you go back to the beginning in which you are naming the colors. After an extensive time in which you are teaching all of the main colors, then you go on to the third step in which you are refining the first two steps. For example, you would have the child make a color wheel and shade the colors from dark to light.

This three-step process occurs naturally and spontaneously. That is the very reason that children all appear to be geniuses. Indeed, they are! If we as adults had to assimilate the vast volumes of information that a young child does, we would collapse from exhaustion. Young children are learning at an incredibly rapid rate, never again to be repeated. They are constantly taking in data via multisensory modalities, organizing and assimilating it. So why do problems occur when the child goes off to school?

Schools often do not teach in the way that children best learn. Most schools teach for visual tract learners. These are the children who learn best by seeing something. They are usually good readers, can quickly grasp things that they see, like worksheets, workbooks, and such things that schools like to dish out. Now this is fine for children who are visual learners (approximately one-third of all children). Most *teachers* are visual learners and so they teach visually and thus schools continue to be havens for visual learners.

Ah . . . but what about those other children? A smaller percentage of them are auditory learners which means that they need to hear it *and* talk about it to assimilate information best. Talking usually goes on in the teaching process, and these children can grasp the subject at that time. But when they go back to their place for "seat work," suddenly it is all "Greek" to them. It is vital for them that a teacher or parent patiently explain the subject matter to them again and allow them to verbalize what they are learning. With a patient parent or teacher they can survive school.

But wait a minute. Almost one-half of all children need to touch something to understand it. They can often cruise through a preschool or kindergarten program because the teachers use many things for children to touch, or at least the children have lots of playthings to touch. But then first grade hits and suddenly, these children have a problem. Why? Because they cannot learn as well with just visual or auditory input. They *have* to touch and there is nothing to touch except a book, pencil, or worksheet and frankly, those don't count as kinesthetic learning tools!

Suddenly Johnny is a behavioral problem. Susie is biting her nails or wetting her pants. What is a parent to do?

When you know what kind of learner your child is, you can gently ask the teacher if you may observe the class. Be careful not to put the teacher on the defensive. But make an attempt to observe whether your child is being taught in the way that he or she learns best.

First, let's identify what type of learner your child is.

♥ *Visual Learners*

1. They need to see something to understand it.

2. They often roll their eyes up and to the right or left as they are being talked to because they are trying to "picture" it in their mind.

3. They like to write things down.
4. They need quiet in order to concentrate.
5. They can handle a lot of visual input like charts, graphs, pictures, etc., but usually like it orderly for maximum concentration.
6. They generally learn to read easily unless, of course, they have dyslexia.

On a personal note, I am a visual learner. I need to see it. I tell people, "Please don't tell me things to do when you pass me in the hall and expect me to remember. Write it down for me." It is no accident that the first book I published is called *A Gift of Time,* a time management system, full of places to "write it down." It came from my own life experience. Visual learners tend to do well in the traditional school scene and so it's no accident that I have been a teacher, school principal, Christian education director, and author. I love to read and I love to write. I am a visual learner in every sense of the word.

Our youngest son, Christopher, is a visual learner like me. Our desks have to be in perfect order and things have to be quiet before we can concentrate. Noise and activity give us headaches. We thrive on quiet and order. We love to read. We love to write. We think best when we are alone.

💜 *Auditory Learners*
1. They need to hear something to learn it best.
2. They like lots of auditory input.
3. They like to tell you things in complete detail.
4. They love to talk and often have to tell you their entire day in sequence.

For children who are auditory learners, we should minimize visual *distractions.* Let them talk. Let them tape-record things and listen to them.

My husband Paul is an auditory learner. Listening, for him, is a complete and intrinsic experience. He plays in the Dallas Symphony Orchestra. He loves for me to attend his concerts. For him, listening to a concert is a complete experience. I love music and I love to hear the orchestra, but I can't just sit and listen. I read the program, study the people, and then often become very creative. If I can't write down these ideas as they come, I get very frustrated or, finally, sleepy. So, in the name of domestic bliss, I found a compromise. I put my time organizer into my purse and then when the ideas come, I jot them down.

All was well in the Capehart Kingdom until that fateful night when he asked, "How did you like the 3rd movement?" To which I promptly replied, "Great! That was when I did my best planning." Whoops! Our marriage did survive, but we do acknowledge our differences.

Angela is like her daddy. She loves a lot of auditory input. When she was a baby, we noticed that as the noise level went up, she perked up. At age two, when we took a family ride at the fair that left me "green," she was undaunted and said, "More please." When I clean her room to my level of "perfection," she says it makes her tummy hurt. She has to "mess something up" in order to feel good. She loves to sing and learns songs very quickly. Christopher memorizes the written word quickly while Angela memorizes what she hears quickly. Christopher can look at his Bible memory verse and remember it. With Angela, we put it to music and then she remembers it.

❤ *Kinesthetic Learners*
This is probably the most ignored and least understood of the learning modalities. That is because the adult world runs on visual or auditory tracks. As adults we learned to "adjust to the system" and therefore forget how important it is to touch. We think that this is just a part of childhood. Characteristics of kinesthetic learners are:

1. They need to touch it.

2. They may seem hyperactive and are often labeled as such because they are restless and frustrated when they can't "touch it."

3. Attention Deficit Disorder (A.D.D.) children need kines-

thetic learning and do calm down when they can touch things.

4. They learn best by doing and interacting with the item.

5. They need to minimize their visual and auditory input and just work alone with a "hands-on" item.

Damon, our oldest, was A.D.D. and thus very kinesthetic. But as he got older he began to acquire auditory as well as visual skills. For example, his mind is like a tape recorder and records things perfectly as auditory people often do. However, he does not focus in, and unless you *ask* to play the "rewind" button in his mind, he doesn't hear what you said. So, he has *learned* to write it down to help remind himself. He is learning to manage his A.D.D. by strengthening his weak areas. This is, after all, what learning is all about.

Damon tends to be more auditory than visual. You often find that to be true of kinesthetic learners. Auditory and kinesthetic often go together as a combination. One day, he asked if he could listen to music while he studied. Since he is so "unfocused" as a general rule, I said no. I felt that it would be another level of distraction for him. My husband suggested that I consider "practicing what I preached." So, since auditory learners love auditory input, I said reluctantly that we would try it out. I was most surprised to discover that the music helped him focus better on his schoolwork.

The best learning environment, of course, is one in which all three learning modalities are in place. If a child can do three learning modalities simultaneously, learning is maximized.

Now let's go back to your specific problem with your child. First, observe your child to see which type of learner he or she is. Then secondly, observe in the classroom. If your child is an auditory learner and the teacher is giving him volumes of worksheets, he may be having trouble. He is not learning in his comfort zone. Ask the teacher if he could take a tape recorder to class and tape some of the most important lectures or teaching times and go back and listen to it at night alone or with you.

When you go in to meet with the teacher, be gentle as you

approach the subject. I have spoken to school and church teachers around the country, and I am continually amazed to learn that even though teachers know that children learn in different ways, they do not teach correspondingly. Good teachers want their students to learn. That is why they chose this profession. But they may need to be educated in how children need to be taught through the different learning modalities. Teachers often have many demands placed on them and they get overwhelmed at the thought of teaching all three modalities and individualizing their teaching. You, the parent, can be a support to them. If you tell them that you will work with your child to facilitate the teacher's job on the home scene, you often get better results.

There is yet another factor involved in the learning process and that is the learning style.

❤ Learning Styles

Learning styles are the *processes* through which a person learns. There are characteristic *patterns* for each style. The following four learning styles are based on the work done by Bernice McCarthy in the 4MAT system (Excel, Inc.). I have changed the names of two styles to tie them more closely to typical learning characteristics as well as learning modalities, and temperaments.

❤ Rita the Relational (Innovative) Learner

Typical characteristics of the Innovative Learner include loving to talk and relate to the learning process. Marlene LeFever calls this particular style "relational," and I prefer that name as well.

Rita functions best when she can talk about it, relate to it. Thus Rita is the sister to the Sally Sanguine personality. The minute you say, "Let's talk about it," Rita perks up. "Now you're talking my language," she says. The truth is that Rita would talk in any language and uses her hands emphatically to emphasize that point. She loves to *relate*. She is very loving. She rules with her heart. She's a people person. She probably has the Gift of Mercy as she empathizes, gives, and loves. Or she may have the Gift of Giving as she gives to others so generously. She may perhaps have the Gift of Exhortation as she ministers, comforts, and encourages. Rita wants to know why, and talking is the avenue through which she seeks the answers.

Some guidelines to better manage the Relational Learner include:

1. Give them lots of opportunities to discuss things. In the classroom children like Rita will continually want to talk. They should be provided with positive opportunities to do so and then helped to understand when they need to be quiet and listen or work. At home, set aside time each day in which you simply give them focused attention and listen to them. Since they are often nonstop talkers, you may get tired of their talking and begin to tune them out. But if you schedule time to give them your complete attention, with the understanding that you cannot let them monopolize all of your time, you can begin to teach them some self-control in this area.

2. Provide opportunities for them to encourage and serve others. They thrive on giving. At home, let them make cards and cookies for shut-ins. At school, they could help another child with his schoolwork. Encourage this beautiful gift they have because the world needs more of these people.

3. Do teach them self-control with their talking. Relational Learners need to learn that they cannot always be talking and asking questions. They have to learn when to be quiet and to be a good listener.

♥ Al the Analytical Learner

Al, on the other hand, does not want to talk or relate. He wants the facts. He likes things black and white. His key virtue is wisdom and he rules with his head. He is conscientious, studious, analytical, and perfectionistic. His twin may well be "Melancholy Melvin." He's your "Steady Eddy."

Al may have the Gift of Teaching as he researches, analyzes, and seeks to teach the facts. He may have the Gift of Prophecy as he brings people to state convictions and to face a righteous God. (See Raye Zacharias, *Styles and Profiles*, 1217 Whispering Lane, South Lake, Texas 76092.)

Al is a quieter child. He likes to observe others. He likes to study things and analyze them. He may be critical but he can't take criticism. He may not participate in as much imaginary play as the other children because he is so factual. Al may not have as many friends as Relational Rita, but he is a most interesting child to raise.

Guidelines to help children with this learning style include:

1. Provide opportunities for them to discuss things in their comfort zone which is the objective arena. Remember that children like Al are not comfortable with discussing subjective issues, such as how they feel about something. Slowly help them to get in touch with their feelings and then to discuss them. This will have to be taught, as it does not come naturally. They feel things deeply but cannot articulate them with ease. Sometimes you have to give them the words that they do not possess spontaneously in terms of relating to themselves. For example, this learner could give you a letter perfect definition of the word *depression* but could not verbalize how this could ever relate to his own experience. It is easy for this learner to acquire wisdom, but he cannot always apply this to his personal situation.

2. Provide Bible facts, have Bible drills and contests as well as other factual, learning experiences for these children. This is where they excel, and we want to provide opportunities for them to "shine."

3. Develop a quiet, orderly environment, well supplied with reference books such as encyclopedias and dictionaries. They do not like activity or discussion, they simply enjoy the process of acquiring more factual information. Therefore this learning style usually produces good students.

4. Teach these children people skills since they often do not have them spontaneously. They have to be taught how to

relate factual information to real-life situations. They often grow up to be good teachers of intellectual information or research analysts but can become workaholics to avoid interacting with people. Gently teach them people skills and remember that this is very difficult for them, so be patient!

❤ *Ken the Commonsense/Kinesthetic Learner*

In the Learning Styles Inventory, Ken is called the "Commonsense" learner. I prefer to call him the Commonsense/Kinesthetic since he is so much like the Kinesthetic modality learner.

Ken is a "hands-on" learner. He wants to know "how it works." He is a loner. He does well with independent projects. He is tenacious. He is impulsive. He sees a need and quickly responds. He seeks justice and wants things to be fair. He may have the Gift of Serving because of his willingness to respond to a need.

To help this learner:

1. Provide lots of opportunities for them to touch as they learn. Children like Ken are definitely more Kinesthetic in their learning processes.

2. Realize that they work best alone. Don't pair these children with another or expect them to play well with siblings. These children do best when left alone. They will stick with a job until it is complete, often to the exclusion of everything and everyone else in their world.

3. They see a need and respond quickly to meet that need. In this sense they can be excellent servers and this should be encouraged. They can often "bite off more than they can chew" and can become overly committed. Like the Analytic, they can become workaholics if not trained to let some things go. They are servers like the relational learners, loners like analytical learners, but completely unique in that they stay to themselves. They are hardworking, action-oriented, "Do it NOW!" kind of people. Give them an independent project or a problem to solve and get out of the way because they are well on their way to solving it.

4. Define what they can and cannot touch in the environment. These are the children who will take things apart to see how they work. They are not malicious, simply curious. They have to be taught appropriate times and places in which to take things apart.

❤ Dan the Dynamic Learner

This is your leader. He is the visionary, the C.E.O. He thrives on activity and likes to do sixteen things at once. He likes to get his hands on things, and much like Ken the Kinesthetic, may often be like a bull in a china closet. He charges, and then aims. He may have the Gift of Administration as he enjoys setting schedules, policies, and guidelines. He may need to learn sensitivity. He sees the parent as superfluous since he knows he could run things just fine. He responds well to you letting him be in charge of something. Like the choleric, he only hears the words *in charge*. Since he loves activity you can put him in charge of most anything action-oriented, such as taking out the trash, cleaning up the leaves, etc., and get good results. This is your leader, so raise him wisely.

Some helpful guidelines for managing this Dynamic Learner at home as well as at school include:

1. Have lots of things for children like Dan to *touch* that can keep them busy but calm. Legos are wonderful for these children because they can touch and create while remaining relatively calm and quiet. This is much better than giving the child a toy gun because the gun would tend to encourage him to be overly active. These children many times finish their schoolwork quickly and need something to play quietly, such as a map puzzle, math game, or even Legos. Having things ready for this child to touch will provide much needed quiet for the classroom or the home.

2. Let them be *in charge* of something productive. Use those very words. Let it be something you choose, or give them two things to choose from. For example: "Sam, you may be *in charge* of taking out the trash or keeping up with

all the outside toys. Which do you choose?" Remember, they want to have control, so give them limited control in which they think they have made the decision, but in reality, you have defined the parameters.

3. *Change the routine* frequently because they become easily bored. Obviously, certain routines are necessary for optimum home and classroom functioning. But find areas where you can provide change for these children. They thrive on it.

4. Dynamic learners are always thinking, *what can this become?* So provide a stimulating environment which they can explore to answer that question for themselves. Again, have lots of things for them to touch. These children want to find out the answer for themselves. Children with this learning style can grow up to be great leaders since they are so production and goal oriented. You don't ever have to motivate them, their switch is always "ON!" You need to help them temper that drive with inner discipline and sensitivity. Pray for this child to be a godly leader.

♥ Loving Our Learners

As we look at the different ways in which children learn, it is easy to see why parenting is so difficult. Each child enters the world with his own completely unique script and purpose. That is why it is impossible to state simplistic rules for parenting and expect them to work for each child. Parenting, like teaching, must be approached on an individual basis. The Bible provides excellent guidelines for raising children to be godly adults, and we can all benefit from the wisdom gained from the Word. But we must also see each child as the unique creation that God intended him to be, especially designed for God's ultimate purpose. God knows His purpose for your child so He is the best source of information on how to raise that child. "If any of you lacks wisdom, he should ask God who gives generously to all without finding fault, and it will be given to him" (James 1:5, NIV). Pray continually to be the parent God needs you to be for your child.

❤ *Parent Participation*

1. What learning modality do you most relate to as an adult?
Visual? (You like to see it and have things written down.)
Auditory? (You need to hear and talk about it.)
Kinesthetic? (You thrive on doing and touching.)
2. Circle the learning style that best describes you? Why?
Dynamic Doer
Relational
Analytical
Commonsense/Kinesthetic
3. In what ways can you see that your learning modality and style impact the ways you parent your child?
4. What learning modality is most comfortable for each of your children?
5. What learning style most accurately fits each of your children?
6. How can you best work with your child at home to facilitate his/her learning needs?
7. Do you think your child's learning needs are being met in the school environment? If not, what can you do to facilitate the process and work with the teacher?

THREE

Enriching Your Child's Environment

Try an experiment. Walk around your home on your knees and observe your environment closely. You will be amazed. You will see things you have never seen before or at the very least, your perspective of your home will change dramatically. This is how your home looks to your child. What can you do to enrich this environment? What can you do to facilitate and maximize your child's learning process?

Before we begin to look at the environment, let's take a look at the child himself. We must remember that every child is an *individual*, uniquely patterned for God's purposes. And every child needs to develop as a *balanced* individual. If one part of him is developing too rapidly, it may be at the expense of another. For example: the child who is sky-rocketing intellectually is often paying the price emotionally. Wise parents will enrich their child's environment to facilitate growth in the following areas:

1. physical
2. emotional
3. mental
4. spiritual

💙 *Physically Enriching the Environment*

Order. Young children (18 months to 3 years) are in the process of ordering and organizing their environment so they can integrate all the information coming in via their senses. If we provide "a place for everything," this helps a child organize his environment.

You may be saying, *Are you kidding? You haven't seen my child—there's not an orderly bone in his body.* Try this. Pick out his five favorite toys. Put them on a low shelf, with a clearly designated place for each one. For example:

You may designate the proper place by using one of the following systems:

a. a *picture,* such as from a catalog

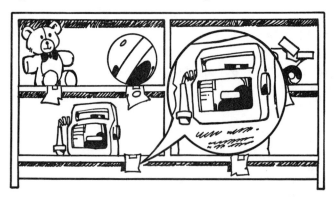

b. a colored *dot* or *shape* on the shelf and the same colored dot or shape on the toy.

As the child learns to match and line up the geometric shapes and/or dots, he is learning more levels of organizations.

c. a *word label*

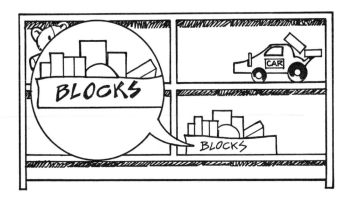

You may add more items to the shelves when your child can handle putting these five items away. But be prepared for a delightful surprise. Your child will start putting your things away as well. Be careful, it may be your newspaper, your "important" papers, favorite shoes, or even your car keys!

As a child experiences order, he will want more order.

Believe it or not, children have a very strong need for order, especially around ages two to three.

Categorize. Separate loose items into containers so your child learns to *categorize*. Again, label the box, code it, or put a picture on it. If things get out of order, sit down with your child, line up the boxes, and reorganize. If you verbalize as you go, you will have provided the most wonderful "hands-on" lesson in organizing. You will reap rich dividends in laying the foundations for teaching your child to be an organized learner.

A word to the wise: start simply. Begin with a few mainline toys such as:

1. Stackable rings
2. Pegboard
3. Stacking tower
4. Simple four piece puzzle

Graduate to containers such as:

1. Crayons
2. Blocks
3. Trucks/cars
4. Figurine dolls

Do not overwhelm or complicate the situation by providing too many items or too many containers. Slowly add items as your child demonstrates that he can effectively organize and care for them.

I suggest that you *not* buy toy boxes. They teach nothing. A child simply learns to pull out, play, and throw back.

Instead, purchase low shelves and put them in different rooms of your house. This communicates to your child, "You are a very special and integral part of our home. You belong here." You can purchase inexpensive shelving that comes with five stackable shelves. These can be placed strategically around your home. For example:

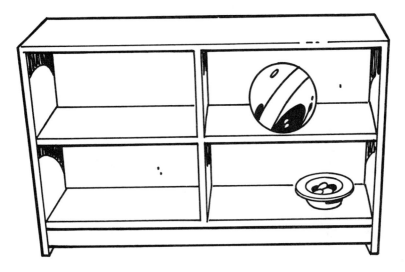

Color. We all respond to color, whether we are aware of it or not. Bright red stimulates us, and may even overstimulate us. Blue soothes our spirit and has a calming influence on us. Green and light peach have been used by hospitals because of their healing effect. Yellow is a mentally stimulating color.

Research shows that the primary colors are better for babies because they are easier to discriminate. Many parents have responded accordingly. Yet so many of us still prefer the pastel colors for our babies. Why? Perhaps because the pastel colors are so soothing to our adult spirit.

Color is a fun concept to play with. Play color games with your child. "I wonder what an elephant would look like red." Color different colors in a coloring book instead of just the traditional and expected color choices. Get a prism and look at different colors. Paint rainbows in different order. Let your child's color creativity abound!

You can also enrich your child's environment with color. For example, if you have a Choleric Carl or Dynamic Dan, you may want to "calm them down" some with a quiet blue or green room. Red, yellow, and orange may be too stimulating.

Your quiet, withdrawn and perhaps moody "Melancholy Mel and Analytic Al" may do well with the cheery stimulus of soft yellow. Red and orange may be too irritating to them, and blue and green may pull them deeper into themselves.

💜 Emotionally Enriching the Environment

Provide a warm, loving, nurturing environment. Remember to touch, love, and affirm each child. Praise the child's *attempts* to learn and master the environment. Appreciate his uniqueness. Strengthen your faith by trusting that God made this child the way He wants him for His purpose. Yes, this child is in need of training and guidance, but his unique design came from God.

Children are like sponges. They absorb what is around them, physically as well as emotionally. As we examine what we have placed in our children's environment, what message are we sending? What do we want them to soak up? To absorb? To mirror back?

If we yell, how can we expect them to be quiet? If we hit them frequently or are abusive in anger, how can we expect them to be gentle and loving? If we are verbally abusive, how can we expect them to reflect back a positive self-image?

Children are born mimics. It is often easy to spot behaviors that children have learned from their parents. For example, men who are gruff in expressing their feelings often produce little boys with the same body language and mannerisms. One day I was in the home of a friend who lamented that her little boy didn't seem to show any respect for her. When I saw the way her husband treated her in front of the child, I realized that until her husband changed and modeled a better attitude, the child would think that it was OK to treat his mother with little respect. Unfortunately, that child will probably grow up to be verbally abusive to his wife and the cycle will continue. Remember, patterns of emotional response are generally formed by the time a child is five, and it takes many years and much hard work to change these patterns.

❤ Mentally Enriching the Environment

Realize two very important and distinctive differences in the way that children and adults perceive *work* and *play*. Adults often work for a living and play to relax. For children *work is play and play is work*. A paradox? Let's explore this concept.

Children are close observers of the adult world. They imitate what they see. As they dress up, cook dinner, hammer nails, and mow the lawn they are very happy. They do not perceive this "work" as a tiring process.

The work of the child differs profoundly from that of the adult in its purpose, procedure, and production. The work of the adult is usually to produce something *external* in the world whereas the work of the child is to produce *internal* results. The work of the child is to create the skills necessary to build the adult he is to be.

It is wise to create an environment filled with child-size "work" as seen from the adult world. For example, provide orderly ways for a child to learn how to properly:

1. Fold clothes
2. Set a table
3. Hammer a nail
4. Make bread
5. Prepare food

We may categorize this as "work" and think that a child needs to go to his toys to play. However, for a child who functions best when he can experience his environment via all of his senses, this work and play are synonymous, especially when he is allowed to explore and discover on his own.

Likewise, the very process of playing is part of the work of childhood that constructs the inner person. Just as children imitate the work that they see adults do, they also play back real life situations, both happy and sad. As they play these experiences, they slowly integrate reality into their understanding.

To illustrate this point, let's take a child who has just had a very painful and unexpected shot at the doctor. The well meaning adult in her life whom she trusts completely has said, "This is good for you. But it will sting for a minute."

Within this communication are many vague words that are meaningless to the child at this level of her understanding. *Sting? Minute?* Too vague. *Good?* Oh, good, that's a nice word. She hears a semi-comforting tone in the adult's voice. But she feels stress. Lots of confusing signals. Then, whammo! Here comes the shot. *Ouch! It hurts like crazy. This is for my good—are you kidding?* She looks at the adult and mistrust may set in. Now what?

A child needs to integrate this painful, confusing experience into her own level of understanding. How can she do this most effectively? By *playing* it back into her reality. Observe her. She may pretend to be the doctor or nurse first and give her stuffed animal or baby doll a shot. She verbalizes those silly nonsense words and may add a few of her own. She integrates the pain and confusion into her own life experience and in so doing reduces the pain. She takes a situation in which she had no control, puts herself in the driver's seat, and recreates the scene. Each time she does this, the stress level is reduced. Play heals.

Allow opportunities for creative, imaginative play. Let your child talk to himself, to imaginary friends, and with his toys. Play is healing. Children will often say more to a puppet, animal, or doll than they will to an adult. Don't stop this creative process in children. It is as constructive as work is.

Enrich the environment with books. I cannot state strongly enough the profound importance of reading to your child. Read to your child from the day he is born.

Reading is rewarding for many reasons, including:

1. Holding your children closely is always a plus.
2. Allowing your children to hear the patterning of the language even before they can understand or speak strengthens their ability to master language skills.

3. Teaching your children to create pictures in their minds and to see the relationship between the written word and images strengthens their ability to read.

We are *not* reading to our children so they will read early. I am not encouraging the "Teach Your Baby to Read" mindset. Reading should be done to enrich, encourage, involve, and develop our children's language skills.

Provide a wide variety of intellectually stimulating activities. By this I mean items that challenge the child's mind but are still age appropriate. I do not mean to imply that you need to provide every gimmicky toy on the market guaranteed to raise your child's IQ.

We do not want to create an academic pressure cooker for our children. We seek to provide a variety of life-based experiences to help us better discover how God created these unique people. As we provide music, books, puzzles, and stimulating activities, we learn how God gifted our children. A word to the wise: while we seek to challenge our children to be the most they can be, we must be careful not to rush them. We do not want to overstimulate and overeducate our children.

Dr. David Elkind, in his books *The Hurried Child* and *All Dressed Up with No Place to Go* clearly articulates the dangers of giving too much too soon. That is why a balance of work and play is so essential. Enriching the environment mentally does not imply that we do every intellectual activity or buy every gimmick or educational toy on the market simply to produce a "brighter" and "better" child. It means that we provide a stimulating environment with a wide variety of things which encourage our children to experience and interact with all their senses, thus challenging them.

💜 *Spiritually Enriching the Environment*

Provide areas where a child can be quiet, reflective, and contemplative. For example, on a low shelf place a Bible (or a picture Bible for a young child) and something of beauty from God's world. A child will spontaneously go and sit there quietly. It seems to feed and nourish his soul with God's peace.

Have posters or pictures that show children being loving, kind, and gentle. Be sure that they are at child's eye level and not at the adult level.

If a child can read, place Bible verses around that will help a child deal with character-trait qualities. For example: "A gentle answer turns away wrath, but a harsh word stirs up anger" (Prov. 15:1, NIV).

When you share these items with your child, do so in a quiet voice. As you communicate love and reverence for our Lord and His world, your child will begin to model this from you.

♥ Learning Modalities and Your Child's Environment

We can ease the stress load for our children by enriching their environment in a way that maximizes their comfort zone—a way that suits their learning modality. After reading chapter 3, you have probably identified your children as visual, auditory, or kinesthetic learners. Armed with that information, you can do much to enrich their environment in a way that best meets their needs. The charts at the end of this chapter (pp. 48-52) give you some specific ideas.

♥ A Potential Environmental Enemy

I heard a wonderful story on my favorite Christian radio station. Since I was in traffic and couldn't "write it down" in order to retain it, many of the story details are gone. But the bottom line of the story was that television is the thief that enters our home quietly and robs us of so much of what we say is valuable to us. What is this insidious thief we call "TV"?

Let's take a look at this presence that we invite into the family room and bedrooms of our homes. What does it contribute to the life we say we want to live?

Let's face it. If we had a guest in our home as obnoxious as most of the messages on television, we wouldn't invite him back. So why do we allow this critter to infiltrate our home?

I encourage you to observe your child's behavior without television and then after he has been watching television. Is he disoriented? Do you have to repeat everything? Does he welcome a creative activity, or does he just want to "do nothing"? Does he act out the characters and/or violence displayed on television? Does he have a sense of reality and a creative imagination, or is he always in the fantasy land created by television?

In regard to your family: has watching television taken the place of real family interaction? Is your time together spent watching the tube or do you talk, share, play games, or go on outings? If your only sharing is watching television together, you can eventually become numb to the needs of those around you that may need nurturing. Perhaps the best thing that might happen to your family is having your television break down, forcing you to spend time getting to know each other again.

Now, what are the POSITIVES that television can offer? Educational channels provide wonderful programs for adults and children. How about watching a special together and then turning off the television and discussing the topic or going on a family outing to obtain more information about the topic? Use television positively for occasional entertainment and educational purposes, but don't abuse it. As a family, sit down with the television guide and decide which programs you are going to watch. Don't just have it on all the time as an emotional crutch.

Remember that young children's minds are like sponges. They absorb everything. Sit down and critically watch a program they are watching with that thought in mind. What are they absorbing? Violence? Commercials that say you need sugar for energy and bigger and better toys in order to be happy? Language and lifestyles that do not reflect your family values? Sometimes we see our children act or talk in a way that we find totally inappropriate. You ask, "I wonder where they learned that?" Chances are it was from the television or a friend who is allowed to watch too much television without parental guidance for selection.

With the increase of both parents working outside the home, long drives in traffic and the hectic pace of the world today, it is tempting to just "turn on the tube and zoom into zombie land." But please, don't let the television be your tranquilizer or your child's baby-sitter.

God created us to be cocreators, and it is in utilizing this creative energy that we are happiest. Do more creative things with your child—paint, work with clay, read books, go exploring! There are so many exciting things to do, and you will be so much closer to your child by sharing in the process. One last work: please don't put a television in your child's room. Let his room be a haven of creativity, rich with THINGS TO DO or a quiet refuge to just BE QUIET AND THINK. A room that nurtures your child's creativity will give you a child who can learn to be happy alone and think for himself. His work at school will improve because his mind is more stimulated. You will also have a happier, more closely knit family. With dividends like these, why not invest in non-television time with your children?

❤ Parent Participation

1. Walk around on your knees and look at your home from your child's viewpoint.

a. Is your home functional for him? (For example, shelves and coat hooks he can reach)

b. Is it child appealing? (For example, some pictures and furniture on his eye level)

c. Is it inviting of his presence? (For example, some of his things in family areas instead of only in his room or in a play room)

2. Can you see areas where you have enriched the home environment to challenge your child:

- physically?
- emotionally?
- mentally?
- spiritually?

3. Are you allowing time for your child to create the person that he is to be as an adult? Remember, children create and construct through play. Are you cherishing and challenging your child through providing an enriched environment?

	Visual	Auditory	Kinesthetic
Physically	1. Needs to SEE lots of things in the physical environment. 2. Needs to have the physical environment be orderly. 3. Make a chart for goals or behavior modification where child can see his progress with a √, * or sticker. 4. Paint the room or add colors that have a positive affect on your child.	1. Needs to HEAR things in the physical environment. 2. Needs to be able to speak frequently. 3. Needs to feel comfortable with the communication process.	1. Needs to TOUCH things in the physical environment. 2. Needs to be able to move within the physical environment. 3. Needs lots of child-developmentally appropriate things to manipulate and learn with.
Emotionally	1. Remember that visual learners are acute observers of visual clues such as facial	1. Praise verbally: "I'm so happy with how you cleaned your room;" "I'm so blessed to	1. Hug, touch, pat, etc. to show love and warmth.

	Visual	Auditory	Kinesthetic
	expressions and body language. Be expressive, but be sure you are communicating the message you want to be communicating.

2. Show facial expressions that suggest love, appreciation, and approval.

3. Display posters that demonstrate character traits that you are trying to teach, such as sharing, loving, and serving. | have you as my child."

2. Articulate your feelings so the child learns the language of emotionally relating to others.

3. Ignore stuttering! It is a stage that will pass in most cases if a child is loved and encouraged through it. Please don't say, "Don't stutter." | 2. Expect that this child will show his feelings by touching.

3. Encourage appropriate ways to show feelings by touching.

4. Be emotionally supportive and accepting of this child's extra needs to move and touch. |
| **Mentally** | 1. Provide lots of mentally stimulating things for the child to look | 1. Provide a variety of things for the pre-school child to listen to as | 1. Provide an environment where child feels free to move, touch, and |

Visual	Auditory	Kinesthetic
at on an age-appropriate level. Things on the wall, on the child's eye level should include: *Pre-school:* a. Colors b. Shapes c. Letters d. Numbers e. Animals *Elementary:* a. Maps b. Cursive alphabet-grade 2 c. Manuscript alphabet K-1st with upper and lower case and item that starts with that sound. Ex: Aa 2. Keep lots of age-appropriate books, games, and toys readily	well as sing and/or talk along with. *Night-time:* a. Lullabies b. Story tapes c. Quiet song tapes *Fun and Movement:* a. Hap Palmer b. Ella Jenkins c. Do-Nut Man d. Sesame Street *Teaching:* a. Hap Palmer b. Childcraft c. Visit a teacher supply store and get acquainted with the interesting tapes available. 2. Play verbal games with your child where he listens, repeats, or responds on his own.	explore instead of being told "Don't touch. Sit still... No..." 2. Provide age-appropriate things for child to touch and manipulate. For example: *Pre-School:* a. Puzzles of letters or numbers IF child shows an interest. b. Let child trace letter or number so he can touch, see, and hear you say the sound simultaneously. *Elementary:* a. Let child write letters in a tray of sand.

	Visual	Auditory	Kinesthetic
	available. 3. Arrange a creative corner with lots of open-ended items for the child to see, pretend, imagine and create with. 4. Check out paintings from the library and hang up for 2 weeks to expose your child to the arts. Point out things for your child to see, help him to "see" art.	3. Build in listening as well as talking skills. 4. Arrange a creative corner where child can make believe, play, and pretend. Allow child to talk to himself as he plays.	b. Let child write letters in fingerpaint. c. Let child spell words in frosting or pudding and then lick his fingers!
Spiritually	1. Put up pictures for pre-schoolers and verses (with or without pictures) that reflect godly attitudes or	1. Play tapes of Bible stories and songs that teach Bible. 2. Read to your child	1. Let child manipulate Bible learning materials such as Noah's Ark, items in God's creation, Bible

Visual	Auditory	Kinesthetic
lessons that you are teaching your child. For example, when you are teaching the 23rd Psalm, put up a gentle picture of a shepherd and a lamb for a pre-schooler. For the elementary-age child, put up part or all of the 23rd Psalm printed so he can read it.	from Bible or Bible-related books.	puzzles, Bible maps, etc.
	3. Allow child to "read" them back to you.	2. Let child make things from clay to represent different Bible verses.
2. Read the Bible and/or Bible-related books, *daily!*	4. Say and sing Scripture verses.	3. Dramatize Bible lessons.
3. Provide time daily for child to "read" and look at books. Encourage appropriate and frequent use of books.		

FOUR

Desirable Discipline

You are shopping at your favorite Christian bookstore, and you run into several of your friends and stop to visit. Meanwhile, your child opens a package of stickers and proceeds to stick them all over the store until the owner comes over and begins to fuss at him and glare at you. In your obvious embarrassment, you grab your child, decide to get "biblical" in front of your friends and not spare the rod one bit! You then grab your screaming child and head for the car. In your fury, you drive home, then spank him one more time for good measure and put him in his room. Shaking, you sit down and have a good cry. Let's see what you have taught your child through this incident. Probably not what you wanted to teach him.

Our children are very sensitive to us. They tune in to our wishes easily. They sense our frustration and this often agitates them. So when we want them to be their "very best," they feel our stress, and the result is often an exhibition of their worst behavior. We react, they respond, and the cycle perpetuates. In regard to the stickers, if the child is young, he may not even realize what he's done. In his mind he thinks he is just playing.

Even as you sit sobbing it's not too late to remedy the

situation. The words *I'm sorry* can teach untold lessons to a child. As you hold your child and go back through the whole experience and talk about what each of you could have done differently, the potential for character growth deepens. Thus discipline becomes true discipleship.

The Bible has much to say about the important concept of discipline. One of my favorite verses is: "All discipline for the moment seems not to be joyful, but sorrowful; yet to those who have been trained by it, afterwards it yields the peaceful fruit of righteousness" (Heb. 12:11). The dictionary defines discipline as training, especially training of the mind or character.

As Christian adults, what should be our perspective on discipline? Basically, our responsibility is to provide the kind of discipline which does more than impose outward control through sets of rules and fear of punishment. The discipline we are striving for should ingrain in our children ways of thinking and behaving based on the absolutes of Scripture. With godly character development as the goal, our motivation to practice desirable discipline takes on an eternal perspective and becomes much more important than simply getting our children quiet for the moment, for example. *Christian character* is the goal of all wise discipline, and not simply *control.* (See 1 Timothy 4:7-8.)

In a world of instant rice, the "one minute manager," and fast food, we all want to learn a quick discipline fix. If control is our goal, we can indeed administer a "quick fix" and "make" our child do what we want. In the short run, this will make us look like good parents, but we will pay the consequences in the long run. On the other hand, if Christlike character is our goal, then we need to prayerfully proceed to learn more about discipline. Our decisions as to how we will handle discipline must take on a deeper dimension than momentarily stopping our child from doing what displeases us. We must also ask ourselves, "How do my actions and decisions affect the character of my child? Are they simply for my good?" For example, a lecture or spanking may lower the adult's blood pressure, but it may do nothing for the child's character development. In terms of discipline, the adult's actions produce the best results when they change the child's *inner* experience, i.e., his ways of thinking about and relating to his world.

After twenty years of being a parent, teacher, administrator, and counselor, I have found the following principles helpful in achieving desirable discipline. But a word to the wise: these do not work as a "quick fix." They must be prayerfully developed with diligence and perseverance. And parents must take into account their own temperament, the specific situation, and their goals.

❤ Dedicate Your Disciplining to the Glory of God

We are to make our children disciples of the living God. Our goal should be to raise godly children who live for Jesus Christ, not to simply control our children while they are with us. When we discipline properly, we are helping our children achieve true inner discipline, which will benefit them as well as others. We seek to train our children to be obedient because it is this habit that will enable them to likewise obey God. "Discipline yourself for the purpose of godliness" (1 Tim. 4:7).

❤ Demonstrate the Love of Jesus Christ

Periodically ask yourself, "What would Jesus do in this particular circumstance?" This perspective often changes the way we handle ourselves. Love, especially God's love, isn't just a "gooey-gushy" type of emotion. True love is wanting the very best for that child. I have learned from children that they want our consistent love and not just the emotionally induced "feel good" type of love. As I reflect on what it would be like to be around Jesus, I believe that we would feel that strong, steady kind of love that is affirming in spirit, consistent in emotion, and gentle in physical touch.

❤ Depend on the Holy Spirit

Children test us continually and quickly move us to our limits; therefore, at times we will *want* to run over and grab them and spank them. That is how we *feel.* But when we depend on the Holy Spirit and pray for His guidance, instead of unholy "reacting," we are then capable of wise and godly response. If we take a deep breath, walk slowly to the child, gently cup his face in our hands, look him straight in the eye, and state our desire with a firm but loving voice, he can hear us far better than when we simply yell or swat him.

When we move slowly and quietly and are constantly praying earnestly for the Lord to take over within us, we handle discipline far more effectively. It's the Christian version of "counting to ten." It slows our human reactions down and gives the Holy Spirit a chance to work within us. Again, children learn more from the essence of what we are, than from what we say.

❤ Determine to Be Diligent

Being diligent means humbly seeking ways to better our discipline techniques and persevering in those things we already know even when they are emotionally draining or time consuming. The Bible says, "Whoever loves discipline loves knowledge" (Prov. 12:1). Because the Bible is the greatest source of knowledge, we must be studying the Word of God daily. And we should also read books about parenting, teaching, and discipline. Of course we should be on our knees often, asking God for help to teach the little ones He has entrusted to us.

Being diligent in discipline also affects the way we define our expectations. As our children grow, so do our expectations, but we must be careful that they grow slowly and are consistent with each child's particular strengths and weaknesses. At different ages children require different preparation for discipline. Consider the following assessment.

One-year-olds are in the "dart 'n dash" stage. You cannot expect them to sit for any amount of time. They love to do the opposite of what you say. This is not so much rebellion as a game of "what will happen if I do this?" You must be willing to chase them and remind them often, but be realistic in what they can actually achieve in terms of discipline.

Two-year-olds are actually quite obedient. I do not agree with the expression "terrible twos." Usually, a two year old is upset only if his routine is changed, or he is expected to do more than a two-year-old can realistically do. Two-year-olds do imitate and can easily be trained by an adult modeling appropriate behavior. They love to play games. And almost anything can be made into a game—picking up crayons, making their bed, washing their hands, etc.

Three-year-olds are more clingy. They may whine and need a little more coaxing. But they understand most verbal instructions, like and need adult approval, and can be encouraged into proper discipline.

Four-year-olds: Now is the time we may have a major discipline challenge. Four-year-olds are "out of bounds." They laugh too hard, cry too hard, play too hard—everything is too extreme. This is the age that tries most parents. We need to carefully and consistently define the rules at this age, set the limits, and then take appropriate measures of action when the child needs discipline. We must also be willing to love and accept the child through his extreme ups and downs.

Five-year-olds: They are sweet and compliant and very eager to please the adult. Enjoy it, for the sixes are coming! I think God gives us the grace period of five so we don't consider selling our children on the open market!

Six-year-olds: They are more aggressive and need opportunities to stretch their independence muscles. This is a time to give some positive choices. For example, "Would you like to wear your blue jeans or red pants?" "Would you like to build with blocks or create with clay?"

Seven-year-olds: This is an important time in the development of children. They are moving from being concrete learners to learners who can understand more abstract concepts. They are withdrawing more into themselves at this age. They need our love, support, and consistent discipline.

♥ Decide Your System of Cause and Effect

One of the most effective ways for any of us to learn is reaping the consequences of our actions. The expression "No pain, no gain" says it well. Thus, it is very helpful for parents, teachers, or anyone working with children to sit down and decide what their system of cause and effect will be. Although it is impossible to anticipate every situation with which a child will test us, we can still make a list of general causes and effects. For example:

Cause	Effect
Talking back	Lose special privilege for that day/night, such as a favorite TV show or time on the Nintendo with a favorite game.
Hitting or fighting	Have to apologize to the person. Do something loving with your hands for that person.
Deliberate disobedience	Grounding Spanking

One thing that we have found helpful is to have a jar for each child. If they do something spontaneously kind, respectful, or godly, they get a new marble for their jar. If they obey right away with a good attitude and positive manners, they get a marble. However, if they do not answer with respect, say something unkind to a sibling, or take their sweet time with getting around to obeying, they lose a marble. When they reach a predetermined number of marbles, they receive a reward, such as a special "date" with Mom or Dad. This is not something you would have in place all the time, but use it as a transition activity when some negative habits are creeping in. As new positive habits build in, you wean them off this. Again, Christlike behavior is our goal. I believe that sometimes we can provide something tangible on the *outside* in order to facilitate better inward behavior.

❤ Define Your Basic Rules

Parents need to sit down and ask, "What are the basic rules for our family going to be?" This is a critically important question. Each person comes into marriage with the training from his or her own childhood. He may have completely adopted his parents' system, or she may have completely rejected her parents' system. As a couple, they must now sit down, often with much prayer and discussion, and come up with what they desire for their home life. It is more important for the couple to agree and be consistent with the child than it is for them to come up with the "perfect system." Actually, there is no "perfect system." Parents need to decide what works for them.

For example, my husband and I like our home quiet; therefore, we have a rule that the children cannot run or yell in the house. When relatives come to visit, they always comment on how quiet our home is. Now that doesn't mean noise is bad, it simply means that we don't want a lot of it in our home.

Ideally, rules should be tailor-made to the ages and needs of the family. I have a friend who has four children under age five. She may WANT the rule of quiet, but it is unrealistic. Our children are spread out in ages — we never had two really little ones at the same time. Don't accept someone else's rules as the "right ones." Find what works for your family.

❤ Discuss Your System

After your system is defined, DISCUSS it with family members. Dialogue with them about how they feel about the rules. If your children are older, you may even allow them to be part of the decision-making process. The important thing is to keep the lines of communication open with your children as to how the system operates.

You may say, "Well, I have a strong-willed child who takes great pleasure in destroying whatever system we set up. The more he knows, the more he tries to outsmart the system." I suggest that you throw the ball back in his court. Say, "John, if you were the parent, what would you do in this situation?" (Remember, this is the temperament who always wants to be "in charge.") If your child comes up with a strict and appropriate consequence for his action, say, "That is a great idea, John. You have really made a wise decision. I think we will do just that." Now, if he comes up with a silly, completely inappropriate consequence, you can verbalize, "John, I really think you could come up with a better idea. I guess you're not ready to be 'in charge' of these things yet. We'll try you again later." Believe me, he will work harder the next time. Don't try to break the spirit of these strong-willed children. Instead, learn to channel this strength into more appropriate behavior.

❤ Direct Your Attention

Does the following story sound familiar? You have guests coming in twenty minutes, and suddenly Sarah falls down, or Adam knocks a lamp over, or Jason starts to whine. What's a parent to do? Children are very sensitive to the adult's mood. When we are under the most pressure and need the children to behave the best, they often deliver their worst behavior. Remember the story about the stickers at the beginning of the chapter?

The best way to handle such situations is to simply stop and give your child some focused attention. If we ignore our children, or yell, or isolate them, the problems crescendo and both parties lose. Instead, we must stop and direct our attention to their needs, or if they are young, simply hold them.

Look into their eyes and truly focus on them.

The obvious exception to this principle of discipline is if the child has deliberately done something to hurt another child or has intentionally disobeyed you. You have every right to isolate the child in these cases. Directing our attention is a practice intended especially for the young child who cannot understand why we are so preoccupied.

We must remember that acting up is often children's way to get the adult attention they so yearn for. If we can provide this attention consistently, then our children won't have to go to such lengths to achieve it.

❤ Deal with Details

An old adage states: "Take care of the pennies, and the dollars will take care of themselves." We can apply the same principle to dealing with children. Deal with the details and the big things are often taken care of as well. For example, if we allow children to run and yell in our house, then we need to be prepared for total chaos on a rainy day or when friends are over. If we allow children to "roughhouse," we must be prepared for an injury if someone gets too rough.

Another old adage states: "An ounce of prevention is worth a pound of cure." In terms of discipline, this is certainly true. A helpful way to get a handle on this idea is to think through *when* most of our discipline problems occur. Perhaps it is during dinner preparations. Carefully observe your children at this time for several days. Then make a list of what could be done to make it easier for the children to handle a particular situation. For example:

- Perhaps each child could have a "time out" with a favorite book or coloring book in separate rooms of the house as you prepare dinner.
- Each night allow a different child to help you.
- Maybe this is the special time to put on a favorite video.

❤ *Direct and Redirect Their Abundant Energy*

Children, especially young children, are so incredibly energetic and multisensory. They are fascinated by everything and driven by an incessant curiosity. Some days it may seem that they are "out to get us," but they really are just interested in everything. They learn by doing—and touching.

As an adult caring for young children, we must often direct or redirect them into purposeful activities. It is also wise to child-proof the area as much as possible. This action is far better for the child's self-esteem than yelling, continually spanking, or fussing. Remember, the young child sees everything as open territory to explore and does not distinguish between what is touchable and what is off-limits.

For the safety of a child or another person, some things must, of course, be considered off-limits. A parent may have to raise his voice or slap fingers to get a child's full attention and help him remember that certain things are *off-limits*. These things may include:

- stove
- fireplace
- mother's favorite vase
- babies

If we keep the off-limits list as short as possible, our little ones are more likely to remember the restrictions.

❤ *Demand Good Manners*

We must insist on good manners. The reason for this is because good manners teach so many qualities inherent in the Christian worldview. For example:

- Respect for others
- Concern for others
- Kinder and gentler spirit

Most of us balk inwardly at being ordered around. I believe we need to teach good manners as well as demonstrating them to our children. Verbalizations that get more mileage out of our children may include:

1. "You *may* get ready for bed now." (Instead of "Get in there and get ready for bed.")

2. "Would you *please* put your clothes in the dirty clothes hamper?" (Instead of "Pick up those clothes now.")

I believe children should be trained in, required, and reminded to use good manners, such as:

- "Thank you"
- "Please"
- "May I be excused?"
- "Excuse me"
- "I'm sorry"
- "Pardon me"

❤ *Display Humor*

Why is displaying humor an important principle of discipline? Because without humor, on many days, we could certainly lose our perspective entirely.

Picture this. It's Missions Sunday, and you are going to be introducing the new missionary family in front of the congregation. You have washed and ironed your best outfit. You have the two little ones dressed. And you've nursed the baby. The dinner is in the oven, the table is set, and the dessert is cooling for the special Missions dinner to be at your home immediately following church. You sit the children down to quietly look at books and you hurry to get dressed. You take a deep breath because it's quiet for a moment.

Wait a minute . . . it's too quiet. You rush out to find two very happy preschoolers who have climbed up on your perfectly set table to take a sneak preview of your dessert. As you grab them to minimize the potential chocolate mess, you, of course, get it all over your pink suit. As you drag your screaming two-year-old off the table, he brings your beautiful fresh flower centerpiece off with him.

What are you going to do? You can scream and cry and resent your children, the church, missionaries, and your life. Or, you can laugh. Make it the funny story of the week for your church. Every parent will sympathize. Everyone will laugh. No one will forget this Missions Sunday. Your children will see a laughing, *forgiving, self-controlled* parent. Everyone will be blessed. Thank You, Lord, for humor.

❤ Dignify Each Child

God has made each child with his own special personality, strengths, and weaknesses. Sometimes children may challenge or rattle us. Sometimes we may actually find it difficult to like our own children. So how do we dignify and encourage each child, even when we have these emotions?

The answer lies in prayer. When we turn to the Lord to help us, it is amazing to see what He will do. So many times the Lord has given me grace and love for my children when I did not spontaneously feel gracious or loving. He has helped me find something to praise each child for on a daily basis.

Let us remember that children have feelings. They take orders and criticisms from adults all day. If we had to take all the verbal, emotional, and/or physical abuse that some children have to tolerate, we would be crushed. Let's not crush their little spirits.

Let us preserve the dignity of each child, even in a situation where he did disobey and must be disciplined. Let us choose our words carefully so that we enable him to maintain his dignity and to develop Christlike character.

❤ Disciplining Your Unique Child

Now that you have read about various principles of discipline, let's take a look at how these principles apply specifically to your child. Is your child a visual learner? Does she have a melancholy temperament? The more you understand about your child's temperament and learning modality, the more effective your discipline will be.

💜 *Sally Sanguine*

This is the child who is fun-loving, talkative, and forgetful. Because of these tendencies, Sally will often get into trouble. She is not usually willfully disobedient but just forgetful. Children with this temperament need to suffer the pain of some logical consequences to learn a lesson.

Behavior	Consequence
Continually interrupting and constant chattering.	Start a checklist. Every time she interrupts or chatters, she gets a check. Each check results in five minutes of lost time doing a special activity.
Losing a very nice new coat.	If this has happened before and if she is old enough to be held accountable, Sally may need to suffer the consequence of working to earn a new coat.
"Forgetting" to tell you about very important events until the last minute.	Sally might need to reap the result of missing an event which is very important to her.

You need to be sensitive to the fact that each temperament type will have a tendency toward certain behaviors; however, some of these temperament tendencies, if untamed, can haunt our children for their entire lives. How much better to tame them as children rather than watch them reap a lifetime of painful consequences.

We must also keep in mind that we respond to our children's personality from the realm of our own temperament tendencies. We become a mirror through which a child sees himself or herself. For example, a Sanguine parent may think his Sanguine child is funny, cute, and adorable; therefore, the Sanguine parent may not want to discipline the child when he or she talks continually or does silly things. Thus, the results of a child receiving acceptance from the parent can become a liability in terms of training that child into a more mature behavior. If on the other hand, you are a serious Melancholy, this tendency of your Sanguine child may "drive you nuts," and you may be continuously sending your child a message of "You're not OK. Get serious about these things."

❤ Melvin the Melancholy

Melvin is generally not a deliberately disobedient child, unless perhaps he is part choleric. Discipline for the melancholy child should deal more in the realm of moods or movements. By *moods*, I am referring to the melancholy moods that can at times be overwhelming: "I can't go back to Sunday School because no one likes me." Or, "I can't learn long division, it's too hard." Or, "I can't write a research paper, it makes me suicidal." Melancholies generally overstate things, usually to the negative. These children are overly sensitive and often very conscientious; therefore, when we attempt to discipline them, they may become overwhelmed if we are not careful about our choice of words and actions. Melancholies generally respond well to quiet, relaxed words which call attention to the problem and suggest an appropriate solution.

Remember that melancholies sometimes *move* to a different drummer, and this drummer is very slooooow. Part of this is caused by the Melancholy freeze. This is what happens when the perfectionistic Melancholy looks at the task he needs to accomplish, sees the ideal or perfect way in his mind, and begins to wonder how he can attain that perfection. He begins to doubt himself and thus freezes and cannot function. You need to help the Melancholy child simply *begin* the task to get the inertia going and unlock the freeze. In other words, you "defrost" him into action.

Here are some behaviors your Melvin the Melancholy may manifest and what you can do about it:

Behavior	*Consequence*
"I don't want to go to class, no one likes me. . . . "	Reflect back the feeling, however, provide something that will get action going the other way. For example, "I'm sorry you feel it's unfair that you have to clean your room; however, we believe that it is important for you to learn this skill. How may I help you get started?"
"I'm not ready . . . " (takes an hour to get dressed)	Set a timer in his room. Each day reduce the time by an increment you think he can handle. For example, one minute, two minutes, or five minutes.
	Let the child dress in the car or even be late to a function and suffer those consequences.
Still up one hour past bedtime because it takes forever to do a task.	Let him suffer the consequences of being tired. You don't need to preach; simply say, "Yes, I feel tired when I'm up late also. That's why I need to be in bed earlier."

❤ *Carl the Choleric*

This is the child from whom you can expect frequent disobedience. Sally Sanguine may be sassy, Melvin the Melancholy may be moody, but Carl usually wants control at any cost. This temperament requires continual, strong discipline. Remember, this is Dr. Dobson's "Strong-Willed Child." Don't be discouraged if you lose some battles, but you do need to work hard to "win the war," which is developing Christlike character.

Our own temperaments do influence how we view this process of disciplining our children. A Sanguine parent may try to talk the Choleric child out of his behavior, or try to win him to her side with a pleasing personality. A Melancholy parent will try to control by attempting to parent in the "perfect" way. The Choleric parent will discipline the choleric child in full force, matching will for will. The best way to discipline the Choleric child is to encourage her to "take charge" of her own behavior and then help her channel all this energy into becoming a strong, competent person.

Behavior	Consequences
Tries to control everyone and everything around him.	"You may be in charge of _____ ." (Give specific tasks.) You really can't tire these children out. In terms of ordering everyone else around, you may say, "I am the parent. I make those decisions. But you may be in charge of helping me . . . "
Deliberate disobedience	He must be punished for this. Ask him, "What do you think would be an appropriate punishment? Obviously, if he chooses an inappropriate response, the decision

Behavior	*Consequences*
	comes back to you. Don't give away proper parental control but do *delegate* some to him when he shows he is ready.

❤ *Phyllis the Phlegmatic*

The phlegmatic child is very easy-going. Her need for discipline will usually show up in the area of stubbornness or laziness. But as a general rule, this child appears to be so easy-going that you often don't see many problems. Some areas of frustration may include the following:

Behavior	*Consequences*
Passive aggressive resistance to doing tasks: "Oh sure, Dad, I just forgot. I'll go do it now." One hour later the task is still not done.	If older, allow her to reap natural consequences. If younger, enforce appropriate punishment when a task is not completed within a defined time. For example, if the unattended task only affected her, she needs to go do it and reap the consequences of not doing something she wants to do for that hour. If her neglect affects other family members and this is becoming a habit, you may need to take away privileges such as TV. This is a time when the "no pain, no gain" rule applies.
Stubbornness as a quiet way of resisting authority.	Talk about it, helping child to see it and to under-

Behavior	*Consequences*
	stand how it *can* be sin. Then define appropriate consequences if a child persists in this behavior.

When disciplining a phelgmatic child, define the inappropriate behavior and put time parameters on tasks. Otherwise her sweet, easy-going nature may let things slide and develop negative habits. Allowing phlegmatic children to reap the natural consequences of their behavior as they grow older becomes the most effective way to change that behavior. Phlegmatics resent being pushed by anyone, especially cholerics. But simply letting them feel the pain of a poor grade because the paper was late or suffer the consequences of being tardy for a class will help them to change habit patterns. Don't rescue them. Let them see the need to change their own behavior.

❤ *Vi the Visual*

Vi is the child who processes information visually. She needs to *see* the pattern of logical consequences that follow behavior. If you are a very auditory-oriented adult, it may be difficult for you to communicate and thus discipline the visual child well.

For this child you need to make a *chart of tasks* and let her check them off. She needs to see her progress. Also make a chart listing particular behaviors and their consequences so she can *see* what will happen if she misbehaves.

If you feel that you've "told her a thousand times" and she still won't do it, don't assume she's deliberately being disobedient. You may have an extremely visual learner who needs to be shown and not always told what to do. When you do communicate, use words like *"See* what I mean? I want you to clean your room. Let me *show* you."

Teach Vi how to write things down. This helps her to remember and teaches her a necessary skill that will help her throughout life. She'll appreciate it. When she has a tangible list, then both of you can see what needs to be done as well as what has not been done.

♥ *Audrey the Auditory*

This child can be *told* what to do because she functions well in the auditory realm. This child may be perceived as a discipline problem in school because she is always asking questions, talking, or requiring more auditory input.

If you have an extremely auditory child, and your budget can afford it, buy her a small tape recorder that can fit into a pocket, purse, or briefcase. This little tool could really help your Auditory Audrey to remember, since talking and listening are the two ways she processes information best. She dictates what you have told her to do into her mini-recorder. She plays it back as a reminder. Again, you have created a tight system of accountability, and you have reduced your child's stress load. Both will factor into better discipline.

♥ *Ken the Kinesthetic*

Of the three learning modalities, this is the one that appears to bring on the most discipline problems. This child processes information via movement and touching, so he seems to be "all over the place." This can be very troublesome to a more structured parent.

With these children, I suggest two things. One, observe them to see patterns. As you begin to be aware of their patterns of movement, you will see that it *really* is the way in which they learn and thus necessary.

Second, look into their eyes. You probably will not see rebellion in their eyes. If you do, then you may have to deal with deliberate disobedience. But usually with the kinesthetic child, constant movement is curiosity and problem-solving in action. Please don't punish them for these things. Unless they are touching and moving, their stress level is very high. This child, more than any other, requires a wise and sensitive parent.

❤ Discipleship

Each of us is different, created uniquely for God's purpose. God has given us our children as a part of this purpose. He entrusts our children to us so that we may disciple them and help them to be the very best that they can be. Proper discipline is inherent in this discipling process. It takes time, patience, prayer, and the Word. There are no "pat answers." What works for one child may not work for another. That is why we must view discipline as a spiritual process, strive to be consistent with the Word, demonstrate the love of Christ, and be open to the guidance of the Holy Spirit.

❤ Parenting Participation

1. Write out a favorite verse, relating to discipline, on a 3 x 5 note card. Carry it with you or put it in a strategic place in your home.

2. Sit with your mate and reflect on how each of you remembers discipline being handled in your home. What was the system? How did you respond?

3. Ask your parents how they remember handling discipline. What was the system? How were you as a child? (Yes, patterns persist, and parents usually love sharing this.) How did they discipline you? How did you respond?

4. In view of your child's temperament and learning process, what kind of system should you set up? Define it. Write it down. Communicate it. Live it consistently.

5. Remember that God chose you to be the parent of your child. Be worthy of your calling. Thank Him for giving you that child to raise. Remember, each child is a gift as well as a loan. We don't know how long we will have that child and for what purpose we are training him. But we do trust God's sovereignty and in that trust we take one day at a time. Again, discipline is a *process*. We never *arrive*. We just seek to discipline and train our children to be the very best they can be for Jesus Christ.

FIVE

Communication

Our school is built around a courtyard. During cold weather we sometimes allow the kindergarten children to go through one of the high school rooms as a warmer way to the restrooms on the other side of the building.

One particular day I had to inform the kindergarten children that they could not use that access route. I went over the reason and procedure very carefully and closed with, "Now, children, remember: when you need to go to the restroom, you must go outside around the courtyard."

Later I was in my office, which overlooks the courtyard and, to my dismay, saw a child squatting in the courtyard while his line partner tried to guard his dignity. I hurried out to find out why this child was using our beautiful courtyard as his personal restroom. He must have noted the look on my face because as I approached he said, "But Mrs. Capehart, you said if we needed to use the restroom to go outside around the courtyard!" I had to smile. So much for clear, concise communication. I brought him inside, apologized for not being more specific, and we all survived the experience. I was once again reminded of how very important clear communication is!

💜 *Prenatal Communication*

Where does communication begin? How is it developed? What makes it a success or a failure? I just heard on the news that scientists now believe that much of a child's attitude can be dramatically influenced by the sounds he hears in the womb. I have always wondered about that because of two personal experiences.

When I was eight months pregnant with Christopher, we moved into a two bedroom duplex. We had only the weekend to move and did it all ourselves. So we decided to skip church this one time. I needed more boxes and decided to run by the school. At that time the school was located next to a big Baptist church, and they used our parking lot on Sunday.

I noticed a car pulled close to the front door of the school that seemed quite loaded down. As I entered the school, I heard strange sounds from the sixth-grade classroom. To my dismay someone was robbing the school! I called the police and the person was caught. It was quite a scene for the Baptists! Police cars, a very pregnant woman, and a thief, who clawed the face of a policeman in an attempt to get away.

After four hours I got back home with my boxes and continued the move, thanking the Lord that He had used the one Sunday I was not in His house to worship to His glory and the school's benefit. I thought it was a "done deal."

But that night I began receiving phone calls, "If you press charges, you'll be sorry. We have connections that can hurt you and your baby." We ended up having to get an unlisted number and police surveillance.

I was very nervous, even after the trial was over. Each night my fears increased, and I was afraid this person would do something crazy. But God was faithful, the ordeal finally ended, and Christopher was born.

My son has always had trouble sleeping at night. I have tried everything. We pray together, I scratch his back, read to him for an hour, play quiet music, but he still struggles. One night I asked him to tell me how he feels and what he thinks about during this time. To my amazement, he described the exact same feelings and thoughts that I had during the time after the robbery and during the trial. After I shared with him my experience, we prayed together, and now he doesn't have any trouble sleeping. This experience was a real eye-opener for me.

While I was pregnant with Angela, I taught a great deal of Bible and music. To this day, she wants to be read the Bible or have me sing to soothe her.

I want to follow up on the research being done on this prenatal influence. What a heritage we could give our children by reading them the Word and playing Bible tapes and inspirational music while they are yet in the womb.

We know that our Heavenly Father communicates with us before we are consciously aware of it: "For Thou didst form my inward parts; Thou didst weave me in my mother's womb" (Ps. 139:13).

♥ *Communicating by Touch*

When does the next level of communication come into play? At birth. How do we first hold our child? Are we nervous? Tired? Overwhelmed with love? I believe that those first moments of communication have a strong impact on our children.

I am so pleased that fathers are now allowed to be a part of the birth process—their presence is so much needed and so powerful for the mother as well as the baby. Paul and I enjoy quiet, and so we chose a doctor who would allow a quiet, dimly lit, natural birth with soft music playing. We were so excited to have the birth experience be a peaceful, gentle, loving, and quiet time. But then Christopher had to be taken to Intensive Care and hooked up to machines that beeped and bright lights that were on twenty-four hours a day, seven days a week. I was horrified.

I begged the nurses to let me hold him, to take him to be quiet with me. I stayed around the nurses' station all the time. One night a wise nurse brought Christopher to me. He had not been responding as he should have been in ICU. I held him seven straight hours, nursing him, singing to him, and letting him sleep in my arms. At 6 A.M. she took him back to ICU, to the machines and lights, before the doctor made his rounds. The doctor was amazed by Christopher's miraculous turnaround during the night, attributing it, of course, to the wonders of medical science. The nurse and I knew what really facilitated the healing process. Thank You, Lord, for a wise nurse who knew the healing power of touch.

I share this from personal experience; however, many well-researched studies also document the power of love and touch. So much is communicated by touch.

I always get teased for being the "church hugger." I hug nearly as many elderly people as I do children each Sunday. I find both age-levels reach out easily and respond openly. People in their twenties-to-fifties are more guarded. But the reality is, everyone needs to be touched.

I was thrilled to read about a study on hugs done by Dr. Virginia Satir, a social sociologist. She says, "Hugging transfers energy and gives an emotional burst. We need four a day for survival, eight for maintenance, twelve for growth" (Elise Arndt, *A Mother's Touch*, Victor Books, p. 79).

❤ *Cherishing with a Rocking Chair*

I am a big believer in "rocking chair therapy." I always insist on having a rocking chair close by. I have one in my office, my classroom, and my home. When in doubt, I simply hold a child and rock him. It is amazing what this will do for a child. When my own children are upset, they always say, "Rock me, Mommy."

I believe this simple act brings a child back to the womb experience where everything was still safe. The child had no comprehension at that time whether his parents would love him or abuse him. He didn't know if he would be "normal" or "weird." He simply was enveloped in a warm cushion and rocked continually. From the birth experience on, a child is thrown into conditions which he did not create, and life can be very painful for many children.

Rocking a child soothes that pain. For a while the world is safe again. I love to give that womb-type experience back to a child. Barriers begin to tumble down, tears may come, body language changes, and love heals.

When a child is ready, I look into his eyes as I rock him. I tell him that I love him and that God loves him and that he is very special. Sometimes inner pain will turn a child's eyes away. He isn't ready to hear those words. But in time, love will heal and he will look at me.

There is no fear in love; but perfect love casts out fear
(1 John 4:18).

I made one big mistake in my career as a self-proclaimed rocking chair therapist. I so believed that love and rocking would heal most childhood hurts that I went overboard a bit. As a school principal, when a child was sent to me for discipline, I would rock him. It worked well for me in the classroom, why not now? I would scoop up the child and rock him. I believed with all my heart that if a child felt love, he would not feel the need to act out as much. It seemed easy to me.

So, why did the same child who left my office mellow, at peace with himself, and smiling at 10:00, suddenly reappear at 11:00, needing more discipline? Wasn't my system working?

You guessed it! Getting sent to my office meant loving and rocking! Wow! Neat deal. *Keep acting out and I'll get loved.* These genius children had my number and were working the system perfectly.

Time for plan B. Even though my mothering instincts wanted to kiss away all the hurts of childhood, I had to then learn the love inherent in discipline. I learned how to discipline children and in so doing, I learned a deeper dimension of love.

❤ *Verbal Communication*

The way we communicate with touch is important, but we must be just as concerned about our methods of verbal communication. Children are very sensitive; they "feel" what we are thinking about them. Sometimes it may be we who are having a hard day, but our children may feel they have caused it. Children often feel they have caused a divorce. We must talk with them and carefully articulate what is happening and how we truly feel.

You may be asking, "But what if I really am upset with my child? Will my words hurt his self-esteem?" It is best to communicate authentically. But our words can hurt, so we must select them with care. When we begin to discuss a sensitive issue by saying, "You . . . ," the other person is immediately on the defensive. But when we claim responsibility for how we feel, using "I" messages, then the other person can listen in greater comfort. For example, instead of saying, "You never listen to me. . . . You always. . . . " we should say, "I feel hurt when I tell you to do something and you ignore me. I *feel* like you pay more attention to the television than you do to me." "I" messages become bridges for understanding whereas "You" messages become roadblocks to communication.

Other communication roadblocks include:

- *Moralizing:* "You shouldn't. . . . "If you were a good Christian, you wouldn't. . . . "
- *Analyzing:* "You always say that when you don't want to do something."
- *Judging:* "What a dumb thing to say."
- *Labeling:* "You're acting like you have a learning problem."
- *Threatening:* "If you don't . . . I will. . . . "
- *Advising:* "You should have done it the way I told you."
- *Sarcasm:* "So you think you're pretty smart?"

To avoid these roadblocks and focus on developing good communication with our children, we should practice the following bridge-building techniques:

1. Focus on the *action* the child performed, not the *character* of the child.

"You did a good job of making your bed."

2. Focus on the child's *attitude,* not always the end result of his behavior.

"I can see you tried hard, and I am really proud of you for trying so hard."

3. *Assume* the best in your child.

"I can see you started to pick up your toys. Let's see, which one comes next?"

Communication is that invisible glue that can mend relationships or sticky them up.

❤ *An Environment for Communication*

Before we look at the actual words we use with our children, let's examine the environment that we have provided. Is the emotional climate of our home conducive to caring communication? As we discussed earlier, the unspoken communication of feelings can set a tone for our home. If the words that we are teaching don't match the "feel" of the home, our children will become very confused. Therefore step one is to "clear the air" of any emotional baggage. In other words, let there be authenticity between what we feel and what we say.

The second step is to set aside time *daily* for good communication. I feel very strongly about this and elaborate on it in Chapter 8. Children learn to be good communicators by participating in good communication processes, that is, talking and listening.

Some little children chatter nonstop, and we learn to tune them out. Then when they're older and we *want* to know what they are thinking, they cease to talk. The way to help prevent this withdrawal is to make the habit of communication a positive one in our children's lives.

I make it a habit to meet alone with each child each night just to talk. That's when you really find out what's going on inside your children. They share at mealtime what they learned at school, in the car about what they did during the day, and at prayer time about their prayer concerns. But in this daily time alone, they reveal their innermost cares, concerns, and confessions. I cannot encourage you strongly enough to start NOW in giving your child these daily gifts of your time.

❤ *Parental Communication*

Children can learn much by observing how parents communicate in a marriage and family situation. Paul and I communicated superbly during our courtship. We recognized that we were very different from each other, but we found this fact fascinating. Then as the realities of married life mounted, we found our differences to be annoyances rather than attractions.

Paul and I have found it essential to schedule time daily to communicate with each other. Yes, much of it is about children, home functioning, and responsibilities of family life. Our children observe the process of two people very different from each other finding points of compromise with which we can both be happy. Sometimes it takes a while because we are so different, but we feel the *process* of communication is often more important than the ultimate product or decision.

We also realize how important it is for us to talk about the major issues of life. These shared convictions are what brought us together in the first place, and we need to nurture those times of communication in order to help us get through the day to day realities of life. When Paul and I are alone together, our communication takes on a deeper dimension and becomes the glue that holds us together and keeps us functioning as one in dealing with daily complexities of family life.

💜 Model Caring Communication

One of the best ways to teach our children to become caring communicators is to model such behavior ourselves. Let's examine some of the guidelines for caring communication.

● *Am I being a channel of God's love?*

I challenge you to turn on a tape recorder and record a typical scene between you and your child on one of those "challenging" days. Later, take a box of Kleenex and sit down to listen. Listen first for the tone, the *climate*. Then make two lists and pick out key words you communicated that were hurtful and those that were caring.

In stressful situations it is so easy to revert back to old expressions that were used on us as children. Often we have no conscious awareness that we use them. We have to do some *careful cleaning out* before we can be a channel of God's love.

What else must we do to be a channel of God's love? How can we converse with our family members in ways that best communicate love?

First, we must go to the dictionary of God's love, His Word. We find much there that will help us:

> Proverbs 10:31-32
> Proverbs 15:1
> Proverbs 18:7
> Ephesians 4:29

Then, we must pray to be a channel of His love. As we pray for a heart and a mouthpiece overflowing with His love, He begins to fill us with His Spirit. That is one of the greatest joys of being a Christian. There is hope! The old can fall away and the new can build. "Therefore if any man is in Christ, he is a new creature; the old things passed away; behold, new things have come" (2 Cor. 5:17).

● *Am I living as a Spirit-controlled Christian?*

The Holy Spirit not only fills us with His words, but He

also begins to put a *check* on our impulses. Instead of being a "motor mouth" who has to go back and apologize, we can be Spirit controlled. There is joy in being around a Spirit-controlled Christian. You feel it. You sense it. You desire it.

Being Spirit-controlled means that we can make a conscious decision to *act* instead of always reacting. Instead of bouncing back like a hastily tossed rubber ball, we can begin to control our responses. For example, when I am feeling impulsive and am apt to get myself in trouble, I try to do nothing—which is very hard for me. I force myself to "stop, look, and listen." Meanwhile, inside, I'm fervently praying, "Holy Spirit, help! Take over! Quick!" I muzzle-mouth (Ps. 39:1) myself until I feel His indwelling presence working through me. God is ever faithful. He has promised the gift of His Holy Spirit. He is your forever Friend. He wants to help you. Call on Him! "But the Helper, the Holy Spirit, whom the Father will send in My name, He will teach you all things, and bring to your remembrance all that I said to you" (John 14:26).

• *Are my words characteristic of Jesus?*

Over my years as a school principal, children's pastor, and mom, I have often asked myself, "How would Jesus handle this? What would Jesus say?" I always invite Him to be the unseen guest at parent conferences, staff meetings, and chapel. His very presence changes the climate of any room. We certainly would not act or talk ugly with Him there. This verbalization works well with children also. For example, when our children are bickering with each other in the car, I gently remind them: "Let's leave a space in the back seat for Jesus." It works as an automatic attitude adjuster.

Sometimes when I'm on the road and thinking unChristlike thoughts about the drivers ahead of me, I imagine Jesus sitting in the front seat of my car. Soon I find myself smiling at the drivers around me and praying for them. Drivers are so unconditioned to seeing people smile, they almost go into shock.

• *Are my words considerate of a family member's feelings?*

Do I just "do my own thing" or do I stop and check out how "my thing" is impacting the family?

"Would it be OK for me to vacuum now?"
"Do you need me right now, or may I go type for a while?"

I am convicted of the words, "Hurry is not of the devil, it is the devil." I am at my worst when I'm in a hurry.

I'm working very hard not to be always in a hurry, to take time to "smell the roses" with my children. My success rate is not always high. For example, there was the Sunday my daughter was invited to a birthday party. Afterwards we were going to stop by my office because I had to get some things done for the Missions Conference. The weather was so beautiful after two weeks of rain that we went to the park before we stopped at church. We had a wonderful time. When we got to the church, I was ready to switch gears and "get it done."

Angela was still basking in our wonderful time and wanted to stay right next to me. She decided to write a letter to her best friend. She needed my help on every other word because she was just in kindergarten. I could feel my frustration level rising, but I didn't want to destroy the enthusiasm she had for writing this letter or the mood of our day. Then everyone began arriving for night church, and I was faced with the usual barrage of activities. I began to get more and more frantic to finish my list of tasks. When Angela asked me how to spell another word, I responded, "Well I guess I'm just not supposed to get *my* work done." My daughter's eyes welled up with tears as she said, "I'm sorry Mommy." I felt so crummy. The last thing I wanted to do was hurt her precious eagerness to write her friend. My few words destroyed that delicious warm feeling we had shared all day. I apologized to her, and she forgave me. But I realized that the tenderness of our time was diminished.

Children are often on a much different timetable than we

adults. When I relax and get into their time zone, things go better. Since this isn't always possible I need to verbalize my need for a quicker pace more gently.

When I find myself speaking abruptly to my children, as I did to Angela that day, I have to go to them and say, "I'm sorry. I didn't mean to hurt your feelings."

It warmed my heart one summer day when I was pulling my children around on a raft and Christopher yelled abruptly, "Not yet, Mom. We're not ready." Angela jumped off the raft and quickly swam to where I was and said, "Mom, he didn't mean to hurt your feelings. We're sorry. We do appreciate you pulling us. . . . " *Thank You, Lord, that they are learning to imitate my apologies and not just my abruptness.*

Under the *consideration canopy* I want to cover another issue. Those of us who are called to the ministry must be careful not to assume our family is equally thrilled with this calling. We must be *considerate* of what our calling does to them.

I resigned as school principal, even though I still had two children in the school, because I didn't want them to resent the school as taking their mother away from them. The first day we walked out those doors at 3 P.M. instead of 6 P.M. was one of the greatest memories for all of us.

The same applies to church. If every Saturday morning the children are at the church preparing for Sunday, we had better make it special for them. My children are my special helpers and very important to me. I couldn't do without them. So I "bookend" our time at church with doing things that are important to them. My prayer is that they will see the joy of serving Jesus, become effective leaders who *serve others,* and continue to love church.

We play "Mission Control" before we leave the church each time. We seek out the clutter and messes people forgot to clean up and clean them up. We make it a game and see how quickly we can "divide and conquer" each room. Sometimes they say, "Mom, I'm too tired" or "I need to do my homework" or I sense they simply want to play. I try to be sensitive and *considerate* of their needs because it would hurt me deeply if my children tired of the church because it tired them out. I want to cherish their love for the church and challenge them to be leaders in it.

• *Do my words convey how very much I cherish my children and my spouse?*

> "We are so blessed that God has chosen you to be the head of our household."
>
> "God gave us a very special and beautiful gift when He gave you to us."
>
> "You bless our family so much with your sense of humor."
>
> "I love to hear you play the piano."

• *Do my words contribute to calm or chaos in my family?*

When we speak softly and gently it helps our children to speak that way. When I speak calmly and quietly to my children during hurried times, it helps them remain calm and focused. If I say, "Hury! Hurry!" and I am agitated, then I am just adding to the chaos. Proverbs 15:1 reminds us: "A gentle answer turns away wrath, but a harsh word stirs up anger."

• *Am I composed?*

Once again, we need the Holy Spirit to help us by filling us with the fruit of the Spirit. When we confess a bad attitude and pray for His help, grace abounds. We find strength and peace to handle the daily trials and frustrations of life.

At certain times in my cycle as a woman, I am more easily annoyed. At those times it *seems* that my family has held a special summit meeting to plan ways to best annoy me. I feel like they are out to get me. When I stop and realize that perhaps *my* attitude may need some adjusting and I apologize, then I discover my family seems less intent on annoying me. When I pray, "Lord, change ME," somehow everyone else gets better too.

• *Am I cheerful?*

Do I treat my mate as my date? Do I use the same tone of

voice on our children as I do on our neighbors? Let's practice using a cheerful voice on our family members and see what happens. We can change a whole situation around for the better simply by changing our tone of voice and the choice of words we use to express ourselves. A statement like, "I feel overwhelmed when there are lots of things out of place" will get me much further with my husband and children than demanding, "Why can't you ever put things away?"

● *Do I show concern for each family member?* Is it reflected in my tone of voice as well as in my words?

> "I bet it was hard to be in school today after the baby cried all night."
> "How did you feel when you got your report back?"
> "Are you doing OK about losing your favorite purse?"
> "I know you get a headache on days you have a substitute teacher. Here, let me rub your head."

We must try hard not to add the twenty-five cent lectures about, "If you worked harder, you would have gotten a better grade." Or, "This is the nineteenth purse you've lost this year. Why can't you. . . ?" Try compassion. It builds communication.

● *Do I compliment my children's efforts as well as their achievements?*

It's their *character* that's most important. Some children are gifted achievers, but if we continually praise their achievements, their character development may lag. When we praise children for displaying godly character or for trying to be Christlike, we build in them strength of character.

Be cautious about such statements as, "You're such a good boy," or "You're always sweet." A child starts thinking, "If she knew the truth about me, she wouldn't say that." Anxiety sets in. Praise the deed, the effort, or the character displayed.

For example:

> "I liked the way you shared your toys with our guest." (deed)
> "I know you worked hard on cleaning your room." (effort)
> "I am proud of you for telling the truth even though you knew it might get you into trouble." (character)

● *Am I constructive?*

Some people love to criticize and control and thus can rationalize all their criticism as being "constructive." But in reality, criticism can hurt deeply and children often receive a great deal of it. The tenacity of a two-year-old is often diminished by the onslaught of well meaning criticism from adults.

For example:

> "Now say it better, Johnny. Slow down. Come on Johnny...."
> "You broke Mommy's things again. Why do you break everything?"

● *Am I specific in what I seek to communicate to my children?*

The best advice is: *never assume.* The best illustration of this is the opening story of the chapter.

Another favorite story of mine is the one about four-year-old "Sanguine Sam" who never listened in chapel but always talked about his adventure at Grandma's, etc. He had an uncanny ability to sidetrack any chapel lesson; therefore, I often chose not to call on him during critical times in chapel such as during the Gospel presentation. I knew he would take us on a quick detour to Grandma's, the zoo, the park, or his favorite TV show.

During one chapel message I taught the verse, "In My Father's house there are many mansions and I go to *prepare* a place for you." I was just preparing to give the Gospel message when Sam's hand shot up. I groaned inwardly, trying to ignore his hyperventilating and hand waving. Finally, I looked at him and for once he seemed focused. I took a deep breath and called on him. He said, in his great four-year-old voice, "Mrs. Capehart, Jesus can fix anything, right?" I was in shock. He was reasonably close to the right topic. Another deep breath. "Yes, dear. Why do you ask?" "Well, the Bible says Jesus said, 'I go to *repair* a place for you.' " Once again, I learned the importance of *clarity* in communication.

❤ Parent Participation

There are so many factors that make up good communication. Let's take time to reflect on all the aspects that make up good communication with our children.

1. What are your real *attitudes* as you communicate? What are your real motives? Do you have hidden agendas? How do you really feel? What do your children feel from you? What do your attitudes communicate?

2. What is your *appearance?* What message are you sending your mate and children if you always look "tacky" around the house? If you don't view your body as the temple of the Holy Spirit, how can you train your children to respect their bodies? What does your appearance communicate to your children?

3. How about your *actions?* What do you actually *do* about what you say? Let's be sure that our actions are consistent with our words.

4. Write down some *actual words* that express the attitude of your heart and the type of communication you want with your children. Memorize a few verses that express the spirit of what you want your communication with your children to be. Don't forget to pray about modeling good communication with your children.

SIX

Self-esteem

After having two boys, my husband and I were thrilled to have a baby girl. We both have thick, curly hair and so we were surprised to find that we had a bald baby girl. We were even more amazed to see that she was still bald at age one.

When she turned two and began getting some hair, I found myself exclaiming, "Your hair is so pretty!" I tried to put in the pretty bows and ribbons that I had been saving. Finally, at age three a few of them would stay in her two inches of hair. My delight was obvious.

At age four I noticed my daughter frequently brushing her hair and fussing over it. To my embarrassment, I realized that I had fostered this quirk by talking about her hair so much. I began, instead, to tell her what a loving child she was. Her interest in her hair began to diminish, and she began to be aware of being more loving. The lesson is obvious: children reflect and focus on whatever they see is important to their parents.

Dr. Dobson says that low self-esteem is a problem with which many people suffer. I could not agree more. As I observe people, I see the issue of self-esteem at the root of most successes as well as most failures.

💜 Childhood Experiences and Self-esteem

I was asked to do a seminar on self-esteem in children. Before I began my research, I asked myself what factors from my own childhood had nurtured or damaged my self-esteem.

1. My parents were very affectionate. Consequently, I have always found it easy to be affectionate. In fact, I touch people without realizing it and often have to be careful not to come on too strong with a person who may feel uncomfortable about touching. Touching is natural to me and an integral part of who I am.

2. My parents expected me to be "good." I wanted to please them as well as other adults and so I tried to be "good." I had a silly side which occasionally got me into trouble, but I was never considered a "bad" child. I worked hard to live up to their expectations of me as a "good girl."

3. I was not a cute child. I had a very lazy eye which sat in the corner. I could not breathe through my nose until I had an operation, so I always had my mouth open. As a result, I often looked retarded. To this day, I struggle with a lack of confidence over my physical appearance.

4. I was not a fat child. I was very active and in all my childhood pictures I see a trim child. But my brothers called me "Fatty." It was a nickname and I didn't take it too seriously until one day I was introduced to an elderly woman. She said, in my presence, "She's a pleasantly plump child, isn't she?" I was horrified. I began to fixate on being "fat." I thought about it, talked about it, and worried about it. I remained slim until my junior year in high school and then began to spread out. To this day, I struggle with self-esteem in this area. I am aware that I use food as a "feel good" and reward system.

5. I once overheard my mother say, "Jody is always honest. I never worry about her in that regard." Whenever I wanted to tell a white lie, I remembered my mother's words and did the honest thing.

6. I always liked taking care of children. I got many

strokes for that, and I was a popular baby-sitter in town. I took it seriously and did it well. My parents always said, "She's a born teacher." Is it any wonder that I chose teaching and raising children as my professions?

When I realized how my early childhood experiences shaped my adulthood, I became concerned about the messages my own children were receiving. Where would they end up? Here's what happened in one case.

I was the World Champion Thumb Sucker. As I entered the upper elementary grades, I became more self-conscious and embarrassed by this fact. I remember painfully requesting to go to the restroom when in reality I just needed a thumb break, away from the taunting eyes of my peers. Therefore I watched my own children carefully to see if I had passed along this not so wonderful quality. I was relieved to see that Christopher did not inherit these "wonderful" genes. Angela, however, was the Queen of Pacifiers. When she relinquished her title at age two and a half, I thought we were on safe ground. But two months after she tossed aside her pacifiers, ("They're for babies, Mom.") she discovered her thumb. At her age I thought it was imitative behavior and would be easy to train away. (No, not imitative of me! I did finally give up my thumb.) But the genes were right there and a new world-renowned champion was in the making.

What was interesting to note was my reaction. She had such a pretty smile but with that thumb in her mouth, we didn't see the smile anymore. My happy little girl now looked sullen with that stupid thumb in her mouth and that is what bothered me the most.

Knowing the trauma I went through trying to stop sucking my thumb as a child added to my consternation. So I began to exert MY will. "You *will* stop, Angela." No success. The harder I tried, the more determined she became. Finally, the Lord intervened. We were walking down the hall at church and I was muttering, "Get that thumb out of your mouth." A wiser parent smiled and said, "Let her do it Jody. She'll quit when she's ready."

"Yes," I sputtered, "but what if that is on her wedding day?" But the Lord did put a muzzle on my mouth henceforth, and she's gradually letting go. I learned how powerful parental messages can be and how they can affect a child's self-esteem. Somehow her being "OK" in my book had become intertwined with a silly thumb.

❤ Our Goal: Children with Positive Self-esteem

As parents, we all want to give our children the present of a positive self-image, the gift of good self-esteem. Before we examine how we can give this present to our children, let's take a close look at exactly what it is that we are trying to give them.

Positive self-esteem is feeling good about yourself. It is feeling important to someone who is important to you. It is feeling productive and confident that you can handle anything that comes your way. It is feeling purposeful and secure about reaching your goals. *Self-esteem always expresses itself in the way you act, what you do, and how you behave.*

So what are characteristics of positive self-esteem in children? What is this gift we hope to pass on to our children?

1. Children with positive self-esteem will be proud of their accomplishments.

A young child may appear to be bragging on his accomplishments when in reality, he is just being purely honest about how he feels.

"Mommy, look at this neat picture that I painted."

2. They will handle their frustrations well.

A child with a postive self-image will acknowledge that some things in life are truly tough, but he will keep trying. Perseverance is necessary for achieving success with small tasks as well as large tasks.

"It's really hard to tie shoes, but I can do it."

3. They will assume responsibility.

A child with high self-esteem will *want* to assume some responsibility.

"I'll help you."

"I made my bed all by myself!"

"I got my church offering from my bank all by myself."

4. They will act independently and appropriately.

A little child often says, "I do it myself." Children go through a stage of wanting to do things by themselves; however, they often do not have the skills to do the things that they want to do. Then about the time they acquire the skills, they lose the desire. That is precisely why I encourage parents to train children in skills while the desire is strong. This will do wonderful things for self-esteem!

5. They will approach new challenges with enthusiasm.

"Guess what? Tomorrow we are going to learn cursive. I can't wait!"

6. They will exhibit a broad range of emotions and feelings that are age appropriate.

The key here lies in the word *appropriate*. For example, four-year-olds are emotionally extreme. They laugh too hard, play too hard, cry too hard. They love bathroom words. This is appropriate for this age. You still need to train them into appropriate behavior for maturity, but you must remember that they are manifesting appropriate behavior for their age and are not necessarily headed for juvenile hall (even though some days you do wonder). Now if a seven-year-old child acted this way, such inappropriate behavior would need special attention.

7. They will feel that they have a degree of influence over their environment.

Children with positive self-esteem can go into a situation where they know no one and yet feel confident they will make friends. Once again, temperament does play a part. A Sanguine will try to gain approval through a winning personality. A Choleric will use force to take control of the situation. A Melancholy will be overwhelmed and think that no one likes him and that he has no control over the situation. A Phlegmatic will observe quietly and peacefully from the sidelines and not get too uptight one way or the other.

💜 Parental Expectations of Children

We all want our children to be happy, successful children who grow up to be happy and successful adults. Granted, we do not have a great deal of control over some factors that contribute to our children's self-esteem, as we discussed earlier; however, I believe that we can control our parental expectations and verbalizations which also affect our children's self-esteem.

To examine your expectations, ask your mate or a loving friend to give you feedback about your verbalized and silent expectations of your children. The truth may be painful, but it will open your eyes. You may subconsciously be transferring your own childhood pain to your children. We have all seen examples of parents reliving their own childhood through their children or parents trying to make happen for their children what they wish had happened for them.

I do not ever write or speak about something unless I have experienced it in my own life because I believe in communicating with authenticity. But every now and then I will be speaking and the Holy Spirit will take over. I want to sit down and take notes because the ideas are so wonderful! I then have to go back and do the things that He gave me before I can make them part of my own experiences.

This happened to me with the idea I just mentioned. Convicted by the Holy Spirit, I sat down with my husband and discussed our expectations for our children. For me, this was a real eye-opener. In our discussion it became obvious that we were each responding to our children through our own grid of very different expectations. For example, I am very goal-oriented so I reinforce the children when they take initiative and reach a goal; my husband is very easygoing so he reinforces them when they "take it easy." Whew! Our poor children were getting mixed messages. We talked at length about a compromise that both of us could carry out with a degree of authenticity. This was a major turning point in our relationship and in our functioning as a family unit.

I believe that each parent brings to the marriage his/her own temperament, gifts, learning style, and personality. This, combined with life experience, can become one of the reasons people can't get along. Each person assumes that the way he or she was brought up is *the* right way. It is difficult to change. Our dear friends, Rick and Jeri Fowler, love to tell the following story which illustrates the point so clearly. Their first Thanksgiving as a married couple became a battleground because each kept waiting for the other to carve the turkey. In Rick's family the tradition dictated that the woman did it and in Jeri's family the male always carved the turkey. Both believed their upbringing produced the "right way," and they were enraged that the other person couldn't see this obvious truth. It is funny to hear the story, but the reality is that we all do this in different ways, whether obvious or subtle.

As parents, we need to be wise in "training up our children." But we will make mistakes; therefore, the most important legacy we can give our children is to lead them to Jesus Christ because it is through His sanctifying grace and forgiveness that our children can grow beyond many of the mistakes with which we leave them.

❤ The Parental Mirror and Self-esteem

Dorothy Briggs, in her excellent book *Your Child's Self-Esteem* (Dolphin Books, Doubleday and Company, Inc., p. 49) talks about the phenomena of the mirrors. She explains that children see themselves through a psychological mirror. They perceive what they are by the way the people around them respond to them. Children also see themselves through an insidious emotional mirror in which unstated body language messages may be more powerful than overtly-stated messages. For example, the patience or impatience with which we pick up a baby is saying volumes to that child.

These mirrors become powerful mechanisms that help produce our self-esteem. As babies and young children, we are powerless over them, yet all the while they are making us who we will be.

I realized that my focus on my daughter's hair had become the mirror through which she saw herself. The hair was actually just the fun of having a baby girl, yet, to her, it seemed to be the most important thing about her because it was what I focused on. The reality is that her character and personality are far more important to me.

We parents become the mirrors through which our children see themselves. Our verbal and nonverbal expectations become the grid through which they measure themselves. As Dorothy Briggs challenges us in her book, we must find out where we got these expectations and if they are valid.

• Are they borrowed? ("A quiet child is a good child.")

• Are they hangover wishes from our own childhood? Do we become determined that our child will get what we longed for but did not get from our childhood?

• Do we place our current hungers upon our child? ("Be the BEST!")

Children look up to us, and whatever we think is important, they think is important. As Dorothy Briggs states, "Children rarely question our expectations, instead, they question their personal adequacy."

My husband is very athletic and musical. Our oldest son is not athletically inclined. I am very proud of my husband for not putting pressure on Damon to share in athletics with him. Damon had quite obtuse interests as a child and yet Paul went "with the flow" just to show Damon that he as a person was enough. I have always marveled at that. Damon never wanted to do the "normal" childhood things, and most adults thought him somewhat strange. But Paul persevered. Today Damon has an excellent ability with music, and he and Paul have much in common with this love of music.

Our son Christopher loves sports. Paul was able to share sports with him, but Christopher has no great interest in music. A wise parent will encourage activities within a child's comfort zone, abilities, and interests. It is also wise to try to stretch your child by exposing him to many things. But back off when the interest doesn't spark. I think of how Paul could have hurt our boys by insisting Damon play sports and Christopher become a musician. He let them be the individuals that God intended them to be.

As a child I loved to play with dolls and play school. I was not really cute nor was I physically gifted. In fact, I was a klutz and always the last to be picked for team sports. I have a daughter who is physically attractive and gifted in sports. I appreciate those things in her, but I want to guard against putting my hangover wishes from childhood on her and trying to live vicariously through her. I want to allow her to be the way God intended her to be.

❤ *Viewing Children As Priceless, Not Worthless*

In Dr. Dobson's excellent book on self-esteem, *Hide or Seek,* he says that our society has two criteria for measuring self-worth: beauty and intelligence. He documents these two criteria so well that it is frightening to think of bringing a child into the world who does not possess these qualities.

I know that what he writes is true. As an educator I was determined to counteract this and help each child see how very special he or she is. It thrilled me when I saw children whose self-image had been battered become healed and whole in our school.

It happened because we worked hard as a staff to do the following:

1. Pray for and with each child.
2. See the child as the individual God created him to be and teach him in that way.
3. Love, touch, and affirm each child each day.

As parents, we also need to pray for and with our children. We need to pray that God will open our spiritual eyes to see our children as God created them to be and that He will enable us to embrace our children's unique qualities rather than force them into our mold. We also need to love, touch, and affirm our children each day. It's easy to get in a hurry and "just get through" the day. But we need to make a conscious effort to look into our children's eyes and truly make contact. The world can be cruel to our children, especially if they are a little different. In order to find a harbor in the storm of life, our children need the anchor of parents who love them unconditionally.

Children want to please their parents more than anything else in the world. And when they do something that yields parental approval, their self-esteem is reinforced. If a child finds parental approval spontaneously and easily because *what* he is is exactly what his parents want him to be, a positive self-image is born. But pity the child who has "jumped through every hoop," figuratively speaking, and Mom and Dad are still not happy. How his soul grieves. Instead of feeling priceless, he feels worthless. It hurts. And he begins the process of building defenses to ease the pain.

The child who receives parental strokes for what he does, builds upon those experiences. Positive experiences build positive behaviors. Negative experiences build defenses.

To illustrate this, let's look at two sisters. Sara is a Sanguine. She loves people! She's fun-loving and qualifies for being cute and adorable. Her sister Molly is a Melancholy. She's quiet. She observes. She is cautious because she wants to "do it right." Daddy is a Sanguine/Choleric. He thinks Sara is funny and he is always saying, "Come on, honey, tell my friends a joke . . . sing a song. . . . " Sara sees the world as a stage and loves to please. Molly watches Sara and tries to imitate her, but personality-wise she is incapable of doing what her sister does. The father keeps trying to encourage Molly but doesn't see that he is asking her to perform in an area that is not her strength. Sara and Daddy get closer. Sara builds her compensations around her strengths: "You like my joke, Daddy? Here's another. You like my singing? Here's a new song. You like my dancing? Get me lessons, Daddy, and I'll really show you." Sara grows up with a strong self-image and becomes a fun music and drama teacher.

Molly begins to build her defenses around her perceived failures. The key here is the word *perceived.* Molly is not actually a failure, but she feels that way because of how her father perceives her. This brings us back to what Dorothy Briggs calls *mirrors.* Our children see themselves based on how we see them. What do your children see in the mirror of your expectations? Do they feel priceless or worthless?

Let's watch Molly some more to better understand the process of self-esteem. She can't "jump through the hoop" Daddy wants. He's too fun-loving to appreciate her quiet, sensitive spirit. Her heart aches to share her love of poetry and art with him, but his only response is, "Lighten up, Molly, don't be so moody." So up go Molly's defensive walls to ease the pain of her broken heart.

Molly, a bright child, begins to form a plan to get Dad's love. She observes that her sister gets strokes for telling jokes so she buys a joke book and memorizes jokes. She tells them. No one laughs. No one laughs because it's obvious that she memorized the jokes but doesn't think they are funny herself. She tries to sing and dance to the modern music that Sara loves, but it isn't natural for her so everyone is uncomfortable. She retreats to her room and cries to classical music.

She continues to try to be Sara and fails. Her pain and frustration mount as do her father's requests to "Stop being so moody." She withdraws and the second defensive wall is built. Molly sees her own interests in ballet and classical music as invalid because her father doesn't appreciate them, and so she becomes more and more withdrawn, thus fulfilling her father's expectation of her as a moody person.

Because she is continually compared to her sister, jealousy mounts. Molly is now an angry, bitter, defeated young woman. Even her love of classical music cannot soothe her troubled soul. She retreats. No one notices. To get their attention, she decides to try more dramatic means: first a suicide note, then an attempt, finally a success. Her father is sad, but as he said at the funeral, "I never did understand Molly. She

was always so moody." The truth is he never tried to understand her as God created her to be.

This illustration may seem too strong for you. But in reality, these things do happen. When parents do not take time to
look at their children as God created them, disaster can
result.

❤ *ABCs of Self-esteem Improvement Plan*

Now that we've examined what self-esteem is and how, as
parents, we affect our children's view of themselves, let's
look at specific ways to help build our children's self-esteem.

A *Affirm* your children.
  Appreciate them as they are.
B *Believe* in your children.
C *Communicate* to your children that you believe in them.
  Cherish them.
  Challenge them.
D *Discipline* them with loving fairness and consistency.
E *Encourage* them.
F *Follow* through on what you say.
G *Give* gifts of your time to your children.
H *Hold* them often.
I *Impart* to your children how very important they are.
J Pray that they will put *Jesus* Christ first in their lives.
  Joke with them, have fun.
K Treat them with *kindness.*
L *Love, love, love them!*
  Listen, listen, listen to them!
M *Mean* what you say and say what you *mean.*
N *Nurture* your children.
O *Open* your mind and attitude to the fact that God made
  your children differently from you.
P *Pray* daily for your children and your relationship with
  them.
  Praise your children sincerely.

Q Spend *quiet* time with your children.
R *Reassure* your children.
  Reinforce their best attempts.
  Resist the desire to make them "just like you."
S Pray for your children's *salvation.*
  Sing to your children.
T *Teach* them the Word of God.
  Talk, talk, talk with your children.
U See their *uniqueness.*
V Minimize *TV.*
W *Welcome* them.
X Try to *exclude* negative influences that will affect their character.
Y *You.* Give them gifts of time with *you.*
Z Take them to the *zoo.*

❤ Temperament and Self-esteem

Our children need to have five basic needs met in order to feel good about themselves. (Actually, adults have the same needs.)

    ● *Part of*—We all want to be connected to something greater than ourselves. Pray for your child's salvation so that his need for connectedness will be met in Christ. He will feel a part in God's kingdom.

    ● *Position*—Each person needs to feel unique and that he is positionally #1 in being the best "him" he can be. This comes from feeling appreciated and affirmed for uniqueness.

    ● *Power*—Each person needs to feel that he has the innate power to make a difference in the world. This feeling of power motivates him to try. A feeling of powerlessness makes us apathetic.

    ● *Peers and People*—Who are the children our child wants as friends? Who are the people she looks up to? We are all influenced, positively and negatively, by the people around us.

    ● *Positive Experiences*—We all gravitate to where we feel good. If we don't feel good when we are with people or when we are part of something greater than us, then we may seek other influences such as drugs, food, or other pleasures of the world.

An understanding of your child's temperament will greatly enhance your ability to meet these needs for your child. Consider the following chart. (Please note: This chart is only a *tool* to help us better see the differences in our children in order to better understand, love, cherish, and challenge them.)

Self-esteem is fragile and intricate, much like a spider web. It is built with much tenacity and care, but it can be easily torn and damaged.

As parents, we must be wise in how we embrace our children's strengths and weaknesses. We must love our children as God made them. We must communicate that love with our touch, talk, and time. We must be good stewards of what God has given us. We must cherish our children as God has created them and then, in that cherishing love, challenge them to be all they can be.

As parents, we should also realize the painful circumstances our children endure day after day. They take classes in which they are lousy. Perhaps they are auditory learners and all of their teachers are visually oriented. Maybe they are somewhat different and get teased mercilessly. Childhood can be a painful, lonely time.

Our job, however, is not to remove our children from painful circumstances. Instead, we should help them see God at work in suffering. I believe that the greatest of God's servants endured tremendous suffering at some time in their lives. It is the fire that perfects. Show me a person who greased through childhood easily because of sports ability or attractiveness, and I'll show you an adult who may struggle greatly. Show me the childhood "nerd," and I'll show you an adult who is sensitive, caring, and wise. Why? Because pain creates character.

A parent who thinks the best way to demonstrate love is to rescue their children from the inevitable pain of life may

Temperament Tendencies and Self-esteem

	Sanguine	Melancholy	Choleric	Phlegmatic
Part of	wants to be part of a group that approves of her and finds her adorable	wants to be a part of something meaningful that is worth sacrificing for	wants to be "in charge" of any group	feels content with whatever life offers
Position	is fun-loving, enjoys being on stage performing	is perfectionistic, genius-prone, musical, artistic	can see whole picture and plug everyone into the parts	feels OK about self, doesn't need to prove herself
Power	performs for others' approval	insists on doing it "right," doing it "perfectly"	likes to run things, take charge, delegate	may gain power by being stubborn
Peers People	tends to pick the flashy Hollywood type	picks people who stand for something they find meaningful	looks up to those in power greater than himself, wants to rule his peers	looks up to those with quiet but witty ways
Positive Experiences	enjoys performing, being approved of, having fun	enjoys creating, perfecting	enjoys controlling, managing, accomplishing	enjoys the flow—isn't disappointed because doesn't have expectations

inadvertently remove their children's best chances for the "good life." Not the good life in terms of ease and comfort, but the good life in terms of developing a godly character.

♥ *Parent Participation*

We all want our children to have positive self-esteem. What can we do to best facilitate it?

1. *Love* your child unconditionally. Make sure he knows it.

2. *Talk* to your child to help him understand who he is and how he fits into the kingdom.

3. *Listen* to your child's fears and worries, joy and triumphs, and be there for him.

4. Provide a variety of experiences so your child will create *compensating behaviors* instead of walls to protect his pain.

5. Help your child to identify and articulate his *strengths* and *weaknesses.*

6. Make sure he feels a significant *part* of your family, he knows his *position* in Christ, he feels the *power* of succeeding at who he is, the love of *people* and the *pleasure* of a life yielded to Christ.

7. Help your child to see the *gain in pain,* the character of the Cross and the true joy in knowing Jesus. With Jesus at the helm of your child's life, no storm can be too great, no weight can sink his ship. Jesus is the only way to peace amidst the storm. Help him to live the Lord's way.

SEVEN

Raising Responsible Children

Listen to a child of age two and you will often hear, "Me do it. No! Me. I do it." As wise parents, we should encourage these steps toward independence. Even young children can accomplish a surprising number of simple tasks. Let's begin early and make accomplishing tasks fun for our children, and we will create a strong foundation for raising responsible children.

As I've said earlier, children are born mimics. They watch us and copy us. Young children of age two or three will imitate whatever they see you do. Use this desire to teach them practical skills.

As a school principal and children's pastor for our church, I spent a lot of time on the phone. At an early age my pre-school-aged daughter begged to talk on the phone. In fact, we have photos of her sitting on her potty chair with a phone at her ear, "writing" down messages. When she was old enough to talk, I took advantage of her desire and taught her how to:

1. Answer the phone properly: "Capehart residence. This is Angela."
2. Dial numbers for her grandparents, cousin, neighbors, and an emergency.

By age four she could accomplish these tasks with amazing ease. Why? Because I taught her at the time her interest level was peaking, and she was imitating what she saw me do. To her, talking on the phone was fun.

Children learn to be responsible by being given opportunities to be responsible. Start when children are young and it is much easier. The cry of the young child is, "I want to do it myself." Teach him at *that* time. Yes, his skills are limited but his attitude is so teachable. The longer we wait, the harder it is to teach.

Believe your children can learn and begin teaching them now. Start where they are, not where you want them to be. Find a strength and build it up. Build in skills they will have for a lifetime. Involve your children in everything you do, and they will learn the practical skills of living.

💜 Reasonable Responsibilities

Each parent must look at his/her own child and come up with a realistic timetable that best fits the temperament and maturity of the child and suits the context of the home environment. If you have been doing everything for your child, don't expect that you can jump in now with the responsibilities I suggest for that age. Begin where your child is NOW and slowly build in the skills. Don't go too quickly or your child will become overwhelmed and give up. Also be careful not to jump back in and start doing everything for your child whenever he is frustrated. Be realistic and take the necessary time to teach these skills. It is a frustrating process. But the rewards for both you and your child are so great.

When I sought to train my own children, I tried to allow for individual differences. For example, my husband's son came to live with us when he was past the early training years that I believe set the foundation for establishing reasonable responsibility. He was immature for his age, had Attention Deficit Disorder, and could barely focus on any task. It took a great deal of training and patience to get him to do a task.

Christopher, on the other hand, took to organization readily. At age two, we were sorting toys into three categories: (1) Give away, (2) Save for later, and (3) Throw out. He understood this and looked up at me and said, "I wove (love) to oganize (organize) wif (with) Mommy." I have always been able to give him lots to do and he can do it efficiently.

Angela spent time in the kitchen with me and learned to make bread and cook at a young age. That came more as a result of her wanting to be with me. But organization is not her strength. Her idea of cleaning her room is to throw everything under the bed so I will get "off her case."

I work hard at training all three of our children. However, I have to take into account their different abilities and aptitudes. I cannot make comparisons between them because God made each of them differently. I must train them in all of the skills but always remember that children mature at different times and have different strengths and weaknesses. As we build upon their strengths, we help them to become stronger individuals who are more confident in who they are.

Before I offer you specific suggestions for raising responsible children, let me share a few words of wisdom I've gleaned from that wonderful school we call "experience."

1. Teach them gently, step by step.
2. Don't expect perfection.
3. Make it fun—a game!
4. Praise their efforts.
5. Don't redo it!
6. Break it down into component steps. Don't assume they have a skill until *you* have seen it demonstrated.
7. Pray for patience.

❤ Creative Cooking

Begin this when children are still in the baby seat. Put them on the counter with you while you prepare the meal. Talk to them. Kiss them. Help them to feel a part of everything you do long before they can contribute anything. When they are babies let them stir something. As toddlers, put the following out for them next to you in the kitchen:

1. A floor covering for the inevitable mess.

2. A low shelf or table with bowls, measuring cups, water, and spoons for them to stir and "cook." Give them safe things such as cereal to pour back and forth, and stir. They can eat it afterward and think they have truly prepared something.

3. Put a pan of water on a low shelf and let them wash dishes, babies, boats. This single activity will buy you more kitchen time than anything else. First of all, children love to be close to us. Second, they love to do what they think we are doing. Third, water is soothing for children.

● Give them a small sponge and a two compartment container such as a dog dish. Put a little water in one of the sides. Then show them how to soak the sponge in the water, then squeeze it out into the empty side of the dish. They can continue going back and forth. Children love to do this for long periods of time. Remember, it is the adult who thinks you have to be doing something with a definitive purpose. Children do for the sake of doing.

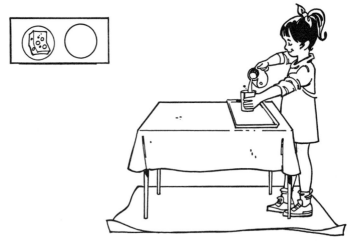

● Give them a nail brush and soap. Show them how to scrub their nails. Then dry their hands. Dump the water out into a nearby pail. Wipe out the pan. Fold the towel.

● Show them how to scrub a table. Give them a brush and soap and water and let them go after it.

In their preschool years let your children be with you in the kitchen. They can learn an amazing amount of skills if you take the time to teach them. For example:

● Stirring.

● Pouring. (Start with small pitchers and definitive quantities.)

● Breaking eggs.

● Measuring. (A perfect way to teach fractions!)

● Cutting up items. Start with bananas and a simple table knife. You can graduate to more difficult things such as celery, bread, apples, and even carrots with a sharp knife. Please, don't panic. Children CAN cut with sharp knives IF you have taught them how to do it. Be right there next to them but trust in their ability. They will amaze you!

● Breaking and washing green beans.

● Washing and scrubbing vegetables and fruit.

● Peeling vegetables. Show them how to always peel away from their body.

Remember, we may think this is work. But little children always think that doing grown-up things is fun. Take them step by step through the process of learning the skills. Don't try this before a dinner party or when you are in a hurry. Take your time. Make it a fun, sharing experience between you and your child. Sing. Talk. Share. Brag at the meal about all your child did to help to prepare the meal. Reinforce participation.

Making bread with children is a wonderful experience that I believe can teach so much. They learn patience. And they learn about yeast and how it is needed to make bread rise. You can talk to them about the Passover and unleavened bread. Leave out the yeast one time and observe what happens. Let them knead the bread, punch it down, watch it rise, shape it all different ways, and put it in different kinds of pans.

I started something which has helped me out time-wise and also helped train the children into what it takes to put a meal on the table. Once a week each person in our family has the responsibility of planning, purchasing, and preparing the meal. Even Daddy has his night! On the younger children's night, I do each step with them. They take their favorite menus and recipes and file them in our family files. We pull the cards for what they want to make and the grocery list is on the back. They learn the many steps involved in preparing a meal. They learn what a bummer it can be to work hard only to have someone come to the table and say, "Yuck! I didn't want this!" They become more sensitive and understanding of how the cook feels. I have said that my sons' future wives will thank me someday for this invaluable training. Do they have to clean up? Yep! That's part of the process as well. But the good part is that after it's all cleaned up, we can have a special dessert personally selected and prepared by the "cook" as well! So we end up happy.

To sum up, little children love to help in the kitchen. What an optimum environment to teach an abundance of skills. For example:

> *Organization:* We take out what we need, and return it to its place.
> *Large to small:* Let your little one stack the measuring cups properly.
> *Order:* We follow the instructions in order.
> *Vocabulary:* Stir, spoon, baste, measure, hot, cold, oven, stove, dissolve, knead, rise, boil.
> *Cooperation:* "You stir this in while I measure the flour."
> *Math:* 1/4, 2/3, 1 plus 1/3. What a perfect way to teach fractions.
> *Care:* "We crack the egg gently and put our thumbs in the middle so we don't get all the little egg pieces in our cookies."

Cleanup: Be sure to teach this very important skill. Again, little children love to copy whatever adults do. You can get a lot of mileage from this. Show them how we clean up after ourselves, and you will have a wonderful helper.

Tasting Party: The best part of cooking is that we get to have a tasting party and taste our creations. But let's train our children to save this until the cleanup time is completed.

❤ *From Bedlam to Bed Making*

Somehow parents think children naturally acquire the ability to do certain tasks. At some point a parent looks at the bedlam we call a bedroom and says to the child, "Clean your room NOW!" The battle lines are drawn. The child is overwhelmed. The wails begin and may not wind down until the parent either gives up or goes in and does it for the child. This is your basic "lose-lose" situation. What's a parent to do?

We must present skills and not *assume* that children are born with them. This takes an enormous amount of patience. For each thing that we ask a child to do, we must break it down into simple, measurable steps, and teach each individual skill. This is how children learn.

My preference is to give young children only one blanket that is also a bedspread. Then it's easy to make the bed—just pull up the covers and smooth them out, one at a time.

For older children, I add a bedspread and show them how to fold it back at the top and then cover up the pillow. (Save the hospital corners on the flat sheet until they've mastered these other steps.)

❤ *From Disaster to Doing Dishes*

We want to minimize the potential disasters that we face in embracing new tasks with our children. What are the components necessary to promote success?

1. Keep it simple.
2. Present how to do it slowly.
3. Allow the child practice time with you right there.
4. Remember, children do for the sake of doing and not necessarily for the finished product. You may want the measurable goal of clean dishes. But children just like having their hands in the water and playing with the dishes. Allow time for this process. Keep things fun and light.
5. Show children the end product so the activity does have a definitive end, but allow time for the process.
6. To minimize the disaster part of it, begin with plastic dishes that children can't hurt. Graduate them to breakable items when the following three factors are present:

> a. You can demonstrate to him how very careful we are with this breakable item. Show him HOW to do it carefully. Children love to imitate us. Dramatically show him how to be ever so careful. The more dramatic and exaggerated you are about the process, the more he will mimic you. You can make this a positive training process.

> b. You are willing to live with the potential consequence of an item being broken.

> c. You are emotionally ready (in other words, in a patient mood) to show your child how to clean up should disaster befall us.

❤ *From Frantic to Folded*

Folding clothes is not one of the things that deeply fulfills many people. It is usually one of those things that we do while watching the news or something else because it's not fun and it doesn't require much concentration. But for little ones, it is an interesting process with untold possibilities. You can let their creativity abound and live with the consequences, or you can train them while they are in the stage of wanting to copy you. Make it a game. Buy some inexpensive washcloths and mark them with a permanent marker like this:

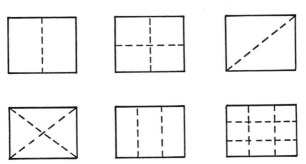

Show your children how to fold on the line. If you are creative, you may want to hem up and embroider some cloths with the same pattern. But the marker on a washcloth will achieve the same effect. These skills of learning to fold horizontally, vertically, diagonally, etc. can be transferred to the many aspects of folding clothes. After the washcloths, you gradually build up your children's ability to fold other items such as:

- real dishcloths
- small towels
- underwear
- T-shirts
- matching and folding socks
- shorts

And so on . . .

♥ Homework Habits

Helping a child learn to organize himself to do homework will help to build a lifelong learner. First, identify your child's learning modality so that you can set up his homework environment to best meet his learning needs. For example, your visual learner will need a quiet place where all supplies are in order. Your auditory learner will need a minimal amount of visual distractions. Your kinesthetic learner will need to be *away* from anything that will distract him, but he needs to have readily available things to touch and manipulate in order to *learn*. For example, if he's learning to *carry* in addition, have Cheerios for him to lay out to show *how* we do it. Have M&Ms to show how we *borrow* in subtraction. Have an apple for him to cut up to teach him fractions. Remember, he also needs a break in which he can move around. Define what you need him to do and then let him know he can have a movement break. But he must reach his work goal first.

Have supplies readily available at your child's desk. In fact, I strongly encourage you to provide a separate desk or homework area for each child. I have also found that it's worth the investment of funds to supply each child with his own age-appropriate supplies such as pen, glue stick, pencils, scissors, ruler, etc.

❤ *Money Management*

Proper training for money management maturity begins when children are young. If we simply give them money everytime they want something, they begin to think we have an unending supply of money. They do not learn the cause and effect of money and the inherent responsibility in learning to manage it properly. Regardless of how much money you may have, you must teach your children the responsibility factor.

How do we teach our children to be good stewards of what God has given us? How do we train them to be mature managers of the money they have?

As in everything else, children learn by doing. So if your child gets $1.00 for his allowance, don't give him a dollar bill, give him ten dimes. Then help him take one of the dimes and put it in a special envelope to bring to church on Sunday. Then encourage him to put another dime in a bank. A child needs to see the complete amount and then take the parts and put them in tangible places.

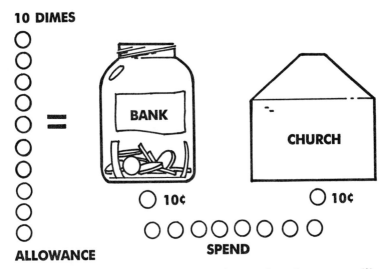

10 DIMES

= **BANK**

CHURCH

○ 10¢   ○ 10¢

ALLOWANCE   **SPEND**

Or you may take three jars and organize the money like this:

CHURCH
(Tithe)

BANK
(Save)

SPEND

As your children get older, their allowances should increase. And as their allowances increase so do their choices about spending it. Don't allow children to purchase something until they have the money saved up or else we will be training them to be credit consumers. We made this mistake with Christopher. He found something on sale that he really wanted, and it was an item that would take a while to save up for. We purchased it for him and let him pay us back. By the time he had paid off the item, he was bored with it and was trying to get us to do the same with another item. It is much wiser to let children save up and see how long the process takes. Then, when they go out and buy the item, they will have a much greater appreciation for the item.

💜 *Triumphant Travel*

Involve your children in the planning of a trip from A-Z, and you will be amazed at the skills they will acquire.

1. Select an outing.
2. Find it on the map.
3. Call to find out the cost.
4. Prepare children for what they will see.
5. Pack a lunch or snacks if necessary.
6. Pack a bag with a change of clothes if you think it's necessary.
7. Count out your money together and put it in an envelope, coin purse, or baggie so your child can pay the admission.
8. Let your child bring a toy, book, or bag of items to do in the car.
9. Talk, talk, talk with your child as you do all of these things: "Do you think we'll need a first aid kit? How about just some Band-Aids? Will we need books to read? Tapes to listen to? Do we have a map?"
10. Organize the car together. Clean it out if necessary. Load it up together. Check the gas gauge. Get gas if needed.
11. Pray for travel mercies with your children before you begin.

💜 *Reasonable Responsibilities for Each Age*

Now that we've talked about some general skills to teach your children, let's focus on specific skills for specific age-groups.

❤ *Suggestions for Children Ages Two and Three:*

1. Make their bed. A word to the wise: keep it simple. Use a comforter type of bedspread that comes up easily. Don't use a complicated one that has a pattern with lots of frills and lace that has to be lined up perfectly.

2. Get dressed by themselves. Help only with buttons or laces that are too difficult for little fingers. Be sure to dress them in clothes that can be put on and off without adult help—this will minimize bathroom accidents. As a teacher and principal, I observed that most bathroom accidents happened when the children had on clothes that they could not get up and down without adult help. Keep clothing simple. This builds self-reliance in children.

3. Brush own hair. Hairbows will still have to be done by a parent, but children can brush their own hair.

4. Brush own teeth. Be sure you have taught them how to do it.

5. Fold clothing like washcloths, underwear, shorts.

6. Put clothes away in their proper slots.

7. Put toys away in their correct places. (See Chapter 3, "Enriching Your Child's Environment.")

8. Clear meal dishes.

9. Set table on a place mat in which you have shown where everything goes.

10. Make a clothing selection from two outfits already picked out by the parent. The child is learning to choose, but you are limiting the choices.

11. Help with simple food preparation such as stir, mix, pour from a small pitcher or container, etc.

❤ *Suggestions for Children Ages Four and Five:*

1. Dust furniture.

2. Vacuum small areas with a Dustbuster.

3. Sweep small areas with a small broom.

4. Clean bathroom sinks.

5. Help clean out drawers and closets.

6. Care for a pet.

7. Polish silver.
8. Help to put groceries away.
9. Wash dishes and dry them. Put away silverware.
10. Make thank-you and birthday cards.
11. Select own clothes to wear. Pack for an overnight.
12. Help with simple food preparation. (See section in this chapter on *Creative Cooking.)*

💜 *Suggestions for Children Ages Six and Seven:*
1. Empty dishwasher. Put away whatever can be reached easily.
2. Take out trash.
3. Keep up with schoolwork and responsibilities such as remembering to bring back a library book.
4. Clean out the car.
5. Practice piano lessons.
6. Write thank-you notes for gifts received.
7. Sweep the sidewalk and rake the leaves.
8. Take shower/bath and wash own hair.
9. Help make lunch for school.
10. Help plan and prepare one meal per week.
11. Vacuum own bedroom.
12. Fold own laundry.

💜 *Suggestions for Children Eight and Nine:*
1. Vacuum entire house.
2. Clean own room.
3. Simple sewing.
4. Simple repairs such as using a hammer and nail.
5. Clean inside and outside of car (with parental assistance at first).
6. Plan, purchase, prepare, and clean up a simple meal with a parent's help.
7. Polish shoes.
8. Iron clothes with parental assistance.
9. Do own laundry.
10. Get own snacks.

11. Learn to budget allowance.
12. Wash mirrors and windows.

💜 *Suggestions for Children Ages Ten to Twelve:*
1. Iron own clothes.
2. Organize own clothes.
3. Organize the bedroom and desk the way that best suits their personality. (This is based upon the assumption that you have already taught them the skills for such organization. Now is the time to start backing off and letting their individual personality come through, even if you don't like all of their ways!)
4. Bake something from beginning to end on their own.
5. Give them opportunities to earn extra money and help them to learn to budget and manage it properly.
6. Plan, purchase, prepare, and clean up a meal on their own.
7. Change own bedding.
8. Teach them about goals. Define them, write them out, set up the steps needed to reach them, etc.
9. Mow yard.
10. Plan and organize a special event.

💜 Reasonable Responsibility for Teenagers

I believe the inward cry of the teenager is the same as the two-year-old: "I want to do it myself." Just as we incorrectly view two-year-olds as being incapable of doing certain things on their own, we do the same disservice to teenagers.

I believe that the more self-reliant the teenager is, the happier he is. Please realize that this statement assumes the child has been raised with a lot of love and praise and trained for these tasks. I have seen homes where children are left alone to take care of themselves for hours every day without a foundation of love and proper training. The self-reliance that develops in this situation is based on survival and is not the same as carefully training your child step by step.

With teenagers you need to look at each skill that will be needed in order for them to move out and successfully take care of themselves. Make a list of all the things that you do as an adult in order to take care of yourself. Make up a timetable to teach each of these skills to your child. If you gradually build these in, your teenager will be ready to be out on his/her own at the appropriate time. If these skills are not well in place, your child will flounder for a long time the first time he is out on his own. The well-trained child can make an easier transition into adulthood.

When my husband's teenager first came to live with us, he had no skills because everything had been done for him. He resented having to make his bed, help with household chores, and take care of himself. It took him hours to do the simplest of tasks because he spent the first two hours having a pity party about how unfair this was. I explained to him that no one likes doing chores—they are simply a necessary part of life. We just learn to do them fast to get them out of the way. This was a surprising perspective to him. It helped to get him going, but the real catalyst came when I said that we were simply trying to help him get ready to live on his own. Now he had a goal that affected him instead of simply doing what he perceived was our "To Do" list.

So as parents, let's cultivate that spirit of training up our children the way we want them to go as adults. Having children do chores is not simply an adult ploy to enforce slave labor (which is how kids often perceive it). Rather, we are training our children to become competent adults, able to take care of themselves.

❤ *Suggestions for Teenagers:*

1. Budget money properly to include money for lunches, clothing, entertainment, and school events. The top priorities need to be tithing and saving. (More on this in the *Money Management* section.)

2. How to take care of a car, which includes keeping gas in it, checking the oil, taking it to the service station periodi-

cally, paying insurance, and all of the other details necessary to keep our cars in proper functioning order. If we do it for them and then send them off to college with a car that they don't know how to maintain, we are only asking for problems. If we train them while they are with us, then we can be there to help if needed.

3. Open up a checking account in your teenager's name so he can learn how to balance a checkbook and keep up with his money. Be sure to open a savings account as well so that the habit of saving becomes ingrained.

4. Teach your teenager time organization skills. Perhaps buy her a simple organizer and show her how to use it to keep up with school and church events, homework, family needs, and her entertainment schedule.

Imagine your child moving into his own apartment tomorrow. Ask yourself: what additional skills does he need in order to do this? Begin training him in these skills today.

❤ *Rewards and Responsibilities*

Young children want to be independent and they want to please their parents. That is why it is so important to begin training in responsibility when they are young. A hug and praise from a parent is reward enough for the young child. As the child gets older, however, he begins to look for something external as a reward. Many parents think this is a negative sign and they don't want to give in to the pressures brought on by a child's question: "What's in this for me?"

Let's be realistic and admit that most adults work for rewards. Our jobs bring us financial reward as well as other tangible rewards. As our children mature, we should teach them about the intangible rewards of serving others without expecting compensation, but younger children don't understand remarks like, "You'll get your reward in heaven." The younger the child, the shorter the time period for delayed gratification should be. Consider the following tangible rewards for responsibility:

1. Time with you.
2. A toy, or something else that the child wants.
3. Money.
4. A shared event such as a movie.
5. A trade-off: "I'll clean your room for you if you cook the dinner for me." The older they get, the more this is a feasible solution. We each have things which we truly don't like to do and others which we can accomplish without too much pain. I think it is fine for children (and adults!) to trade chores.

❤ *Parent Participation*

1. Define what you consider to be reasonable responsibility for your child.
2. What are some age-appropriate tasks that your child could be taught now?
3. What are you doing to help train your child in more skills?
4. List some skills that you would like your child to acquire over the next year.
5. Define your plan of action to help your child achieve these skills.
6. What rewards, if any, do you feel would be appropriate to use as reinforcement as your child attains these skills?
Tangible:
Intangible:

EIGHT

Giving Gifts of Time

One day I called a friend to have lunch and she said she could not come because she was having a "Kristi Day." I asked what that was, and she answered that it is a day in which her daughter gets to choose what they will do all day. I thank my friend Ann McAlister for giving me this idea. I didn't have any children at that time, but I have since used that idea countless times, and it has truly blessed our family life.

A popular phrase is "Love is spelled T-I-M-E." I believe that. A number of years ago I had the privilege of meeting Dr. David Elkind who has written much about not hurrying our children. He did some classes for the parents and teachers in our school, and I was to write up the review for the local newspaper. In reflecting on his talk, two of his ideas particularly struck me:

1. We need to give our children *time* to be children. The world wants them to become miniature adults in their dress as well as in their activities. We need to be diligent in preserving that special time of childhood and in so doing, give them a *gift of time*.

2. We need to give our children our time. Do we give our children quality time or quantity time?

Frankly I was wrestling with these issues of time myself. I had one child at the time. I had kept him in the office with me as a Christian school principal until he was school-age. We were together and yet I was aware that I was often preoccupied. Although we were together physically, he may not have felt my attention entirely focused on him.

Looking around at nonworking moms, I sometimes felt guilty. I did notice, however, that some of these moms had their children in two "Mother's Day Out" programs, two days at the spa child care, and one day at the local church child care for Bible study.

I wrestled and prayed about these issues for several years and these are the conclusions I arrived at for me. There are mothers who stay at home and truly focus on their children and everyone is blessed. There are mothers who think they "should" stay at home, but they resent it and so they have their children in many programs that don't count as "day care" as such but are definitely outside the home. And there are mothers who have to work, and grieve daily over being away from their children. Then there are moms who work and love it and never give a second thought to leaving their child. I observed the children from all of these situations. Who were the children who were thriving?

To begin, I had to examine my own world. I believed my children needed time with me. Quality time is nice, but they also needed time to "just be" with me. They could do their own thing, but they still needed to know I was close.

I began searching for ways to give my children "gifts of my time." This set into motion my resignation from the school. In the meantime, I remembered my friend Ann's idea. I gave each of my children one day in the summer. From beginning to end, I let them choose what was important for us to share together. Gradually, I added more days and time and finally we found a system that works for us.

💙 *Giving Gifts of Time at Christmas*

Seeing how important the "Gifts of Time" were for my children, I made a major change at Christmas and decided to give more of my *presence* and less *presents*.

Presents are transient. Colors, fads, and sizes change. Toys break. But the gift of our inner *presence* is one that permeates and remains forever in our children's memory banks. The *presence* of a calm, happy parent is ultimately a much richer and more meaningful gift for any child. Children are so mesmerized by TV ads and catalogs that they think they have to have one of everything. They "want want want" until they are saturated with desire and totally consumer confused. The season becomes a one-way street with "getting" being the end. I decided to give my children my *presence* as we shared in all aspects of the holiday preparation together.

My Christmas message was "I choose to give you the following PRESENCE this Christmas:

1. My actual physical PRESENCE. I will keep you near me as I am shopping, baking, wrapping, and all the other myriad of things that need to be done. Those of you that are old enough to help can do so. (They were age eight and one the first year we did this. Now they all help with everything.)

2. The PRESENCE of my peace. I will take the time to do whatever it is I need to do so that I can give you my PEACEFUL PRESENCE.

3. The PRESENCE of spontaneous JOY. I will try to laugh with you when things don't go the way we planned.

4. The PRESENCE of my unconditional LOVE. God loved us so much that He gave us His Son Jesus. His love for us is unconditional. I pray that my love will shine even though your ball has just destroyed the centerpiece I have worked on for two painstaking hours.

5. The PRESENCE of PATIENCE when you ask for the one hundredth time, "How many more days until Christmas?"

6. Most importantly, the PRESENCE of mind to always

show you by my example that CHRIST is truly the only reason for Christmas.

I thank the Lord every day for giving me this wonderful PRESENT called YOU and now I want to give my PRESENCE back to you. I love you. Mommy"

This was the first of many wonderful Christmas times together. I love the holidays. I like to start early so as the time gets closer, we can just enjoy the lights of the tree, the smells, and sounds of Christmas. We have established many traditions, which I dearly cherish. For example, we do our Advent Devotion every night with reverence instead of rushing through it just to get on to other things. I want my children to know the PRESENCE of the Christ Child at Christmas and to truly know that Jesus is the reason for the season.

❤ *Weekly Gifts of Time*

Every Friday night I would have a "date" with one of my children. We would do whatever they wanted to do. On very special occasions, we would go out and it would cost money. Usually we would do something at home. Here are some examples of what the kids would choose:

Damon

1. Go to a Christian concert at a local church.
2. Play games.
3. Read books.
4. Listen to music.

Christopher

1. Go to a movie or rent a movie and watch it together.
2. Play board games.
3. Read books and discuss them.
4. Have a deep talk as I scratch his back (his favorite).

Angela

1. Make bread.
2. Take bubble baths by candlelight.

3. Play piano and sing.
4. Put on makeup and dress-up clothes.
5. Have a tea party with Mommy's special cups and saucers.

Angela and I call our nights, "Girl's Party," and the boys call their nights, "A Date with Mom."

Some of the things they chose are activities that we did anyway. But when *they* chose the activity, it became special. They also got to choose the menu for the night and help prepare the meal.

❤ Daily Gifts of Time

The final step in my giving "gifts of time" came when I moved it to a daily event. I began to meet with each child after dinner each night. This is the routine we established:

6:00   Dinner.
6:30   Dishes while they take baths and showers.
7:00   Angela's time: I read to her, go through her day, select clothes for the next day, rock and snuggle, and have devotions.
8:00   Prayer time with everyone.
8:15   Christopher's time: we check schoolwork, pick out clothes, read together, have devotions, scratch backs, and snuggle.
9:15   Damon's time: we used to read, check work, snuggle, and talk. Now that he is seventeen, we just check work and talk.

❤ Taking Time for Reading

I want my children to love to read. I believe that if you read to them when they are young, they will love books. I believe in reading to them from a wide variety of books.

● **Bible** I began reading the little children's Bibles to our children when they were two. This is the sequence that I have gone through for each of my children.

1. *My Picture Bible* by V. Gilbert Beers (Victor Books).
2. *Read 'n Grow Picture Bible* edited by Libby Weed (Sweet Publishing).
3. *Learning to Read from the Bible* series by V. Gilbert Beers (Zondervan). (ages 3-4)
4. *The Picture Bible* (David C. Cook). (ages 4-5)
5. *Illustrated Stories from the Bible* (from Eagle System International). (grade 1)
6. *The International Children's Bible* (Sweet Publishing). (grade 2)
7. *The Bible for Children* (fully illustrated) edited by V. Gilbert Beers and Kenneth N. Taylor (Tyndale House Publishers).
8. *The Illustrated Bible* (David C. Cook). (grade 3)
9. *What the Bible Is All about for Young Explorers* by Frances Blankenbake and Dr. Bob Choun (Regal Books). (grade 4)

We also read from many excellent supplementary books, such as *Little Visits with God,* the Winner Books Animal Tails Series, and the Lion Story Bible Series, *Child's Book of Character Building,* and the *Children's Bible Basics.*

I was not surprised when my nine-year-old son came to me and said, "Let's read the New Testament together from the 'real' Bible this summer, Mom." We are still working on it because we take time to discuss things as we go. I would not give up this precious time with my son for anything.

We have tried family devotions, and we still do them as a family occasionally. However, my husband works many nights and our children are so spread out in age that it simply has worked out better for me to have an individual quiet time with each child. We do pray together as a family a minimum of once a day as well as at mealtimes. Nothing ever gets in the way of this, even if we have company. We just invite them to join us.

● **Library books** We go to the public library every other week. The children select books that look interesting to them. We read one or two of them each day. These are generally fun, easy books and always their choice. I am always looking for books that encourage character building. I buy them for "keepers" in our home library so we can read them many times. Our public library books are generally more superficial and provide light reading, which is important as well; however, one night we were reading a book that caught me by surprise. It was called *The Selfish Giant.* I wept. It was so beautiful. It's not a Christian book, but the love that poured through that book reminded us of the infinite love that our Heavenly Father has for us (1 John 4:10).

● **Educational books** I don't focus a tremendous amount of time here because the children get an excellent education at their Christian school. But for special units of study, we like to get books and read them to spark their interest. Their teachers at Grace Academy read quality literature to them each day and for that I am grateful. We get a list of books each week that are being read to the children in their individual classes.

● **Novels and Quality Literature** I began to read novels to my children at age 5. We began with *The Lion, the Witch and the Wardrobe* by C.S. Lewis. Each of my children loved this book and related well to it. We discussed how we think Narnia would look so they developed the art of visual imagery as they read. I believe this is an important aspect of building strong readers. When we finished, we checked out the video and watched it together. We discovered that this is the only video that matched the way each of us had pictured it in our mind. It was a fun way to draw closure to the first lengthy book we read with no pictures. I believe that it encouraged my children to want to read more novels without pictures. I have treasured the experience of sharing that book with each child. I believe the book also develops wisdom in children as they discover the analogy of Aslan and Jesus. What a rich dimension reading brings to our lives!

We have so many favorite novels that it would be difficult to list all of them, but here are a few titles:

1. All of the *Chronicles of Narnia.*

2. All of the Laura Ingalls Wilder books.
3. All of the *Sugar Creek Gang* books.
4. All of the *Accidental Detective* series (Victor).
5. *Pilgrim's Progress.* (We read it once a year because we love it so much.)
6. *Across Five Aprils.*
7. *Where the Red Fern Grows.*
8. Danny Orlis books.
9. Poetry books.

I encourage you to pick up a book that lists good literature for children, such as *Honey for a Child's Heart* or *Reading Aloud to Your Children.*

I was delighted to see that as my children grew older they wanted to read to each other when I was reading with the third child. They always have a personal book going and read on their own as well. Our home is filled with books. I have seen Christian worldviews deepen as a result of their reading.

I am all for reading to your children as much as possible. I am, however, against the "Teach Your Baby to Read" programs. I believe that puts conditional acceptance upon the child, whereas holding your child close and reading together is an unconditional love experience. Each of my children learned to read almost effortlessly at an early age. I believe that was because they were read to daily and not because of early reading programs. I encourage you to enter the wonderful world of reading with your child. This investment of time will reap rich dividends for you and your child for many years to come. Get out there and discover the treasures readily available for you and your child.

There are so many excellent books on the market today. I am hesitant in sharing any lists of books because I am well aware of the many books I could not list.

♥ Making Time a Priority

How can we as parents give more gifts of time? It begins with better prioritizing our priorities. As I talk with Christian parents, I find that most of them are really busy and frankly have very little, if any, time for themselves. So when we talk about giving even more, it can cause panic to rise up in many wonderful parents. So let's instead take a look at our priorities.

What does the Bible say about prioritizing God's way?

Priority number one: THE LORD. "But seek first His kingdom and His righteousness; and all these things shall be added to you" (Matt. 6:33). We know this. We say it. We sing it. We believe it. But does this always translate back into our lives? Let's take a hard look at the incredible discipline that prioritizing our lives this way requires. The discipline of Christian maturity takes an amazing amount of energy and time. We, of ourselves, cannot do it; we must seek the Lord's help. God isn't going to say at the judgment, "I excuse you from truly getting to know Me because you were busy serving in the church nursery or your mate didn't understand. . . . " Nothing should keep us from putting God first in our lives. The tyranny of the urgent can often creep up on us and keep us from living this as our first priority. Let's begin today to live this most important priority.

Priority number two: OUR MATES. Let's remember to put our mates next. Do we make our mate our date? Do we make special time to just be with him or her? Church, children, and jobs sometimes scream for our attention in ways that our mates do not. Let's not forget that precious person with whom we chose to spend our life. Schedule time NOW so that relationship can be nourished.

My husband works nights and I work days. The good news is that the children are almost always with one of us and we rarely need a baby-sitter. The bad news is that we are often not home at the same time. We have to carefully schedule time to be together or our relationship becomes one of practical functioning and not the deeper level of communicating that brought us together in the first place. Whenever we have time alone together, we remember why we got married in the first place and we cherish that time.

Part of God's school of character building is that He often puts us with someone unlike ourselves. Do we cherish this difference? Or, do we want to "fix" our mates so he or she will be more like us? Do we thank God daily for the spouse He gave us? Do we love our spouse unconditionally? After we set up our daily appointments with God, we need to establish daily talks with our mates and a periodic "date."

Priority number three: OUR CHILDREN. "Behold, children are a gift of the Lord" (Ps. 127:3). Whether a parent is employed outside the home or not, that parent works. The continual "To Do" list of life is overwhelming at times. All parents are busy. Yet scheduling time with our children is a must, and this includes those involved in ministry—as professionals or lay workers.

Our children need to see that their needs hold priority over the needs of others. They also need the security of knowing that we schedule times for them when the world cannot intrude. God bless the technology that gave us telephone answering machines! Such invaluable pieces of equipment allow us uninterrupted quality times with our children.

Priority number four: OUR HOMES. As a wife, I know that my home comes next in the prioritized order of things. A home should reflect the loving care of the woman. There are no rules, however, that say it cannot reflect the extended nurturing of other family members. Our family holds certain priorities that contribute to the functioning of the whole unit.

Priority number five: THE WORLD. Now we can go out into the world to pursue an interest or job and make a difference for Jesus Christ.

In summary, we all spend time with our children. We are giving them gifts of our time each day. But when we package it up with a special name, we have added a new dimension to our presence. Children cherish it. It gives them the personal security to be more of the person God intended them to be. That gift, our presence, becomes the most sought after commodity. Cherish these together times for children grow up all too quickly.

❤ *Parent Participation*

1. How much time do you spend with your children each day? Each week?

2. When was the last time you spent time alone with one of your children?

3. What did you do? Was there time for focused attention in which you were truly listening and not trying to accomplish another task at the same time?

4. When was the last time you did what your child wanted to do?

5. How can you begin to give more "gifts of your time" to your children?

6. Ask each of your children what they would like to do with you all by themselves. Write these ideas down on a 3 x 5 note card. Give them back to your children as gift-coupons that they can redeem with you.

7. Pray for the Lord to help you find more time to be with your children.

NINE

Making Meaningful Memories

My mother has a yellow and white table in her kitchen that she doesn't like. She's been looking for a replacement for some time. At our last visit to my parents' home, our youngest son sat looking at the table reflectively. "Grandma, there are so many wonderful memories in this table." My mom and I looked at each other with tears in our eyes. Suddenly that old table was beautiful. "Beauty is in the eyes of the beholder." Loving, warm memories are often what give increased value to things and people.

Memories can be treasures or instruments of bondage. Of course we all want our children to have warm, loving, meaningful memories. How do we best create them?

💜 Family Traditions

With the breaking up of the family unit and families living so far apart, many traditions have gone by the wayside. It is a comfort to see the Christian world seek to remedy this and now, even the secular world. We do need to start (or continue) traditions for our families.

Traditions are formed by returning to certain repeated patterns, and memories are made by looking back. Thus the beauty of traditions and memories lies in the reflecting process.

Holidays were a source of conflict in our early marriage. When we were dating I asked Paul to go to the storage room and get my *boxes* of Thanksgiving decorations. He, of course, thought I was kidding. He laughed as I decorated my apartment. He laughed when I brought decorations to decorate his parents' house with darling little pilgrims, turkeys, and cornucopias for our first Thanksgiving together. I thought they were enjoying the changes I brought. He told me later they were in shock. Since he was still laughing, I assumed that deep down he was loving the way that I changed my world with decorations for each holiday and season. The truth is he didn't like it, but he didn't make his needs known until we had had several fights during special holidays. I wanted the holidays to be warm and special, and I didn't understand why he was always in such an ugly mood when I was trying to make it the most wonderful time ever. The truth is that I (and all of my "beautiful" decorations) were getting on his nerves. Since celebrating the holidays was at the core of my very existence, I didn't understand him. It took lots of compromising for us to come to a middle ground where both of us could be somewhat satisfied.

❤ *Birthdays*

Remember, I am the one who loves holidays. Paul does let me "do my thing" for the children's birthdays. I really do have fun and try to make the day very special for each family member. Here are some of the ways we celebrate birthdays:

- **Banner:** In our yard I hang a banner or flag that is designed in the birthday child's favorite colors and has his or her name on it.
- **Newspaper:** Over the headline of the day's newspaper, I tape a specially written message such as, "TODAY IS CHRISTOPHER CAPEHART'S BIRTHDAY!"

● **Special meals on a special plate:** The birthday person selects the menu for all three meals that day. Each meal is served to him or her on a special plate.

● **Family time:** We remember and reflect on special things about the person. We verbally cherish this person with our individual memories of this person. For example, we talk about the day this person was born, and then we go on to talk about other special memories.

● **Books:** We enjoy reading special books such as:

a. *The Secret Birthday Message* by Eric Carle (New York: Thomas Y. Crowell Company, 1972).

b. *I Am Your Grandma* (You personalize this book with your child's picture and other related information about his life.)

c. Personalized books that are done on a computer with your child's name throughout. (They love these!) See bibliography for sources.

● **Parties:** I plan and produce the entire party with the birthday person. Several weeks before the party we do the following:

1. Select a theme.

2. Make and mail invitations. The children can invite one friend for each year old they are. For example: five friends for age five party. The only exception to this is that I let each child have his entire school class one year. Once we have had the "big party," we are back to the smaller ones.

3. We go out together (alone) and purchase the necessary items for the party.

4. The day before we decorate the house together, prepare the food, make up the favor bags (items from the Christian bookstore), and organize the games.

I have found that when the children participate in the process from the beginning, they feel more a part of the event. We have learned wisdom together about what works and what does not work. For example, the opening of presents can turn into chaos. So, instead of allowing this complete chaos, I have the children sit on a circle that I have made with masking tape. My child, seated in the center of the circle, invites one friend at a time to bring him/her the gift. When the gift is opened, I take a picture of the two children and the gift. Later I get them developed on the two-for-one special. One photograph goes in my child's scrapbook, and the other goes in the thank-you note to the other child. This makes a nice memory and also makes writing thank-you notes an easier task. In addition, the photographs help my children remember who gave them what.

5. The night of the party we look at each gift quietly and cherish the memory of the gift-giver. We make a list of the gifts and giver while it is quiet. This list goes into my child's scrapbook and we also use it to write thank-you notes. We do this together. Believe it or not, this can be a nice time together and trains children in a very positive habit for life. Then while I clean up, my child can play freely with his goodies. At bedtime we snuggle and reflect on the many blessings of the day. I try to help my child see things other than the toys that blessed his birthday.

❤ Birthday Theme Ideas

Here are some birthday themes that my children have selected and helped produce.

❤ Girl Parties
● *Babies.* This was a wonderful one. We made the invitations with a baby on the front. Each girl was invited to bring her doll. We made diapers for them as the girls were arriving. Then each girl talked to the others about her baby. Then we rocked them and put them down for naps while we had the party. Of course, we had to be very quiet or we would wake up our babies. Because my daughter has a December birthday, party favors were readily available, and we included lots about Baby Jesus. It was one of the easier parties we have done!

● *Dress up.* The girls were invited to come all dressed up with a special dress, hat, gloves, etc. We, of course, had to be quiet and act like little ladies. Again, that made the party quite easy! We made necklaces and pretend earrings. We had a tea party with the good cups and saucers. It was great fun.

• *Angels.* Angela Elizabeth is our little Christmas angel. So we had an angel party. Finding party favors and decorations was easy around Christmastime. We made angels for each girl to hang on her Christmas tree at home.

• *Ballet.* The girls came dressed in leotard tights or a ballet outfit if they had one. We played "The Nutcracker" and let the girls do their ballet. (You could also bring in a ballet teacher or friend who knows ballet to share a little ballet with the girls.) The cake and favors follow the ballet theme.

Before I tell you about parties for boys, I have to tell you about one more girl party idea. Angela received a handmade invitation in the shape of a nightgown. The party was to begin as a breakfast party in the morning and the girls were to come in nightgowns. I thought this was a cute idea, but I really flipped when she came home with a gown that she had made AT the party that looked exactly like the invitation she had received. It even had her name on it. Thank you, Mrs. Nunley, for this darling idea!

❤ *Boy Parties*

Here are the birthday themes that Christopher and I have used.

• *Pirate.* We made the invitations as a pirate ship. We handed a secret treasure map to each child when he arrived, and each one had to begin to search out the clues to find the treasure. The treasure was actually an inexpensive treasure chest filled with gold-foil covered chocolate coins. We turned the table upside down and put butcher paper around it to make it look like a pirate ship (well, sort of). We played the Pete the Pirate song tape which has a Christian message. The boys loved it!

• *Train.* The invitations were in the form of a train. The cake was cut into sections and joined with licorice laces. The wheels were lifesavers. (Each boy could make his own mini-train with cake, licorice, and lifesavers. If the weather permits, and you can gather enough boxes, the boys can paint boxes and build a train in the backyard. (Be sure to put a few drops of detergent in the tempera paint so you don't have unhappy moms.) We had a great time making our cardboard train. Books, games, songs and favors are easy to find with a train theme.

• *Sports.* We set up the house with an indoor basketball hoop, bowling pins, and golf holes. Frankly, this was the most organized party that Christopher and I have ever done, and it ended up being the most difficult to manage. The boys got too excited. Oh well, it was a fun idea on paper!

• *Western.* All the games had a Western theme. For example, they shot out the flames of candles with squirt guns. They loved it!

• *Basketball.* This is our party for 1991, and we plan to do it OUTSIDE. Hopefully it will go better than our sports party, where the kids went from one indoor game to another.

💜 Making Birthday Memories

I made up a book for each child that is a scrapbook called, "This Is Your Life." We look at it together for each birthday.

The children love to take it to school on their birthday to show to friends. It is the "Reader's Digest Condensed Version" of their lives. I organize each book like this:

1. I have their name calligraphed along with a Scripture verse for the inside cover when they are born.

2. I add a verse each year which is the verse I am praying for them. My dear friend Sue Bohlin calligraphs these for me. It is a wonderful record of what key year verses I have been praying for them.

3. I put in key pictures and mementos of the year.

When the children were young, I made audio tapes of them. Sometimes we pull these out and listen to them on birthdays.

I keep a journal on each child and on their birthdays we

read some of these entries. They love to hear some of the funny things they have done.

💜 *Written Memories*

Every mother laments the many things that she *intended* to put in her child's baby book but simply ran out of time. We have all experienced this. Also, I have noticed that children never say cute and adorable things while you are sitting poised by their baby book. Sadly, many of those incredible things that you think you would NEVER forget do slip away from you over the years. This is how I solved the problem for me.

When the children were born, I began one of those *newborn calendars* that has all the stickers for major events such as "first smile." I write only a few words on each square. I leave it above the changing table so it is easy to jot down a word or two. My original intention was to transfer all of this to the baby book, but for the most part, it has just remained on the calendar. I did this for the first two years of their lives because they change so much during these years that each day is important.

When they turned two, I began their journal. This is simply a bound book of blank pages. Any notebook will do, but the hard, bound books with cute covers appealed to me. I write about major events as well as character growth. I also write about challenging times since it is good for a child to see how he has grown beyond certain problems. I believe this builds confidence and helps a child to see that he is mastering many new abilities.

As I said earlier, children rarely save the treasures for when you are sitting by their baby books or journals. They pop those great one liners while you are in traffic or very busy. At the time you are SURE you could NEVER forget it. In fact you think the whole world should know what a precious thing your child has said. You go to tell your husband, or mother, or anyone else who will listen, and guess what . . .

you can't remember. It seems impossible to believe, but it has happened to mothers around the world. What's a mother to do?

My solution was to add a page to my time organizer which is ALWAYS with me. I've added a section titled "Cute and Adorable Things Said/Done." It looks like this:

Cute and Adorable Things Said/Done

Date   Context   He said ...   She did ...

_____

_____

_____

_____

_____

_____

_____

_____

_____

This has saved my sanity many times. A quickly jotted word will help me recall the entire event when I do have a moment of quiet to later enter it into their journals.

💜 *Meaningful Memories on a Regular Basis*

Daily. Spend time with each child reflecting and remembering the day. Read, talk, snuggle, and pray. This becomes a wonderful memory of you that your child will have forever.

Weekly. Do something alone with each child even if it's simply going to the grocery store. Children love to be alone with their parents, and they change when they are alone with us. They are much more mature and willing to communicate what is really going on inside of them.

Monthly. Try to do something special alone with each child that he or she has selected. It really shows how important they are to us when we are willing to do what they want. This does NOT have to cost money. In fact, our best memories are the ones which did NOT cost money. Consider giving coupons to your child, written on a 3x5 note card:

> ❤Angela gets two hours alone with Mommy to do whatever she wants to do.

❤ Meaningful Memories through the Year

Each family needs to come up with special activities that suit family members. The very act of planning these events becomes a meaningful memory. Here are a few of the things we have tried which may work for your family.

❤ January

1. On New Year's Eve or New Year's Day, reflect on the many ways that the Lord has blessed you this past year. Write out goals and prayer requests for the new year. Make a list together of fun things that you would like to do in the New Year as a family. Put this list on the refrigerator and work them into your family time. For example:

- *Adventures.* Make up some neat ones.
- *Books.* Write a list of ones you want to read.
- *Church.* What can we do for our church family as a family together?

- *Drama.* Make up a play together.
- *Etc.* Open-ended items fit here.
- *Games* Decide which ones you want to play as a family.

And so on. . . .

2. Snow Day parties are also fun. Play outside with the children and then come in and make cookies and drink hot apple cider in front of the fire.

💜 *February*

1. Make a LOVE TREE with Bible verses on love.

2. Make homemade bread, kneaded with your love for people that may need a little special love. Put a love message on a loaf and deliver it with your children. Children LOVE to make bread, and this could become an on-going ministry. I think freshly baked bread is one of the nicest ways to say, "I love you."

3. Make Valentine cookies.

4. Make love meals for shut-ins.

5. Discuss things at mealtime about our American heritage.

6. Learn and sing America songs together.

7. Make handmade Valentines for people who normally do not get Valentines.

💜 *March*

1. Celebrate spring. Relate the new life all around us to the new life that we have in Jesus.

2. Celebrate March coming in like a lamb or a lion. What symbolism do we have in the Bible about the lamb? Who did the lion in *The Lion, the Witch and the Wardrobe* represent? Discuss it. Read the book again.

3. Celebrate Easter if it comes in March or wait until April if it comes in April. Discuss why Easter comes at a different date each year.

4. As Christians, Easter should be the most important

event of the year for us. It is because of Easter that we are Christians. It is worth taking lots of time to celebrate this most sacred of days. Select activities that take a longer time to do so that the meaning of the day is heightened.

● *Holy Week Baskets.* Make a basket with your child. Select or make items to go in the basket that represent Holy Week, such as:

    a. Palm branch to represent Palm Sunday.
    b. A small paper towel for Jesus washing the disciples' feet.
    c. A small communion cup and unleavened bread to represent the Last Supper.
    d. Scroll made with two Popsicle sticks and a piece of paper on which your child has written his favorite Gospel verse.
    e. A cross made with Popsicle sticks.
    f. A piece of black felt to show the world turning black when Jesus died.
    g. Grass as a symbol of new life in Jesus.
    h. Shroud cloth.
    i. A rock for the stone over the tomb. Let your child think of additional items.

● *Easter shadow box.* Take a shoe box and add something each day that depicts part of the Easter message. On Good Friday put the lid on the box and don't add anything. For Easter morning, add something special to represent the fact that Jesus is alive and put in a tiny window for them to peek through. See if the children can find the special item.

● *Learn Easter songs* such as "Christ the Lord Is Risen Today" and "I Am the Resurrection and the Life." Even preschoolers like to try singing these songs.

● *Make up tiny baskets* of the following colored jelly beans and put in this poem. Distribute them to unsaved friends. (You may want to add a tract.)

RED is for the blood He gave.
GREEN is for the grass He made.
YELLOW is for the sun so bright.
BLACK is for the dark of night.
BLUE is for the sky He made.
WHITE is for the grace He gave.
PURPLE is for His hours of sorrow.
PINK is for our new tomorrow.
A bag full of jelly beans colorful and sweet
Is a prayer, a promise, and a child's treat.
May the Risen Lord bless you
This Easter and always.

♥ *April*
1. Have fun on April Fool's Day.
2. Celebrate Arbor Day by planting a tree.

♥ *May*
1. Celebrate May Day. I remember this as a lovely time in my childhood and have been saddened to see that most people do not celebrate it. What a lovely time to show caring for others.
2. Celebrate Mother's Day. Let's remember those who have helped care for our children at church or home who may not be a mother themselves and give them a card and flowers. They have been a loving, vital part of our children's lives and may be feeling lonely on this day.

♥ *June*
1. Celebrate Father's Day.
2. Plan a Sizzling Summer Barbecue with your family.
3. Find out what you as a family can do to serve during Vacation Bible School. Make it a special family time.
4. Celebrate Flag Day.

♥ *July*
1. Celebrate our American heritage.

2. Plan a special meal that is all red, white, and blue for the 4th of July. Plan a fun day, including things your children WANT to do instead of planning it all out for them.

♥ *August*

1. Plan for BACK TO SCHOOL together. Buy school supplies together and organize them. Drive by the school, and perhaps you can set up an appointment to meet the teacher and take a peek at the classroom. Remember, make it a short visit. Your child's teacher has lots to do before school starts.

2. Pray about the year together. Be excited about it with your child. If your child has concerns, fears, and doubts, be sure to address them.

♥ *September*

1. Set up a prayer tree together. (See chapter 10.)

2. Find as many fun things as you can to do with apples.

3. Celebrate the great heritage our children have in their grandparents.

♥ *October*

1. Learn more about Columbus Day and celebrate it.

2. Fall fun may include taking wonderful walks to collect leaves. Iron them in wax paper and hang them on your windows.

3. For Halloween, have a LET YOUR LIGHT SHINE FOR JESUS party. Carve out pumpkins with friendly faces and put candles inside to represent letting our light shine for Jesus in a dark and sinful world. Find Scripture verses about the light of God. Make pumpkin bread, roast pumpkin seeds, and have a pumpkin decorating contest. Make sure each child gets a prize for something unique about his pumpkin. Sing songs such as "This Little Light of Mine." Talk about ways to be a light for Jesus in the world. Distribute Halloween tracts. Present the Gospel. The enemy has made this day a nightmare for many families, but as Christians we can make it a great time for evangelism.

💜 *November*

1. Talk to your child about what it means to have an attitude of gratitude. Every time he expresses something that shows a grateful heart and spirit, put a sticker on his chart. At the end of the month reward him with something special to show how important it is to you that he is learning to have a grateful heart. It's great to have a grateful heart. Let's train our children in this attitude while they are young.

2. Make "I AM THANKFUL FOR YOU" cards for those people who often are forgotten.

3. Celebrate Indian and Pilgrim customs. Study up on their lives. Make costumes and invite in someone who doesn't have a family and have an old-fashioned Indian-Pilgrim holiday.

4. Learn about ELECTION DAY. Have an election at home with your children. Have the children research and report for whom they are voting and why.

💜 *December*

1. Try to divert some of the attention from the "getting" and focus on the "giving." This is certainly easier said than done in our consumer world. Here are a few suggestions:

- Adopt a needy family.
- Angel tree participation. (The Angel Tree program is part of Chuck Colson's prison ministry. Information is available in Christian bookstores before Christmas.)
- Give baskets of food to needy families.

Talk with your children about "What do you think would be a good thing to *give* to this person, or to this organization?" Help them begin to think as givers. Build on this attitude.

2. Advent is one of my favorite traditions because it is quiet and pretty. As you light the candles of your own Advent wreath, read from Scripture and talk about what it means to live joy, peace, and love. This all builds to the climax when you light the final candle to celebrate the birthday of Jesus who is the light of the world.

3. Have a birthday party for Jesus for children who may not know the Lord. You could invite neighborhood children, school friends, etc. It may even be good to invite your children's friends who may be saved because this party brings the focus back to WHY we are celebrating Christmas.

♥ Cherishing Childhood

For Mother's Day I took slides of the moms in our church with their children. I sang this song as the slides were being shown as a tribute to Motherhood. I selected this song because, as a mother, it reminded me of how those moments of childhood slip by so quickly. The words challenged me to cherish each precious moment of my children's childhood.

GOOD NIGHT KISS
by Chapmans

I count it as a privilege
I count it cause for praise

To kiss my children goodnite
At the close of everyday.

For I know too soon they're up and gone
And walking out the door

And I'll never have a child
To kiss good night anymore.

It's very strange how times
Have changed from the present to the past
When did they grow so quickly
The time has flown so fast
For it seems that only yesterday
I helped him with his shirt
Or pat my baby on the back

Or kissed away a hurt
Mommy bounce me on your knee
Daddy hold me high.

Let's go outside for a ride
Or make a kite to fly.

— Used by permission

♥ Parent Participation

1. Sit down and reflect for a moment on the traditions that your family had. What do you remember? What part of those memories do you want to bring back for your children?

2. What are some painful parts of those memories that you would like to learn from, release, and thus, not repeat with your children?

3. Ask your mate to answer questions 1 and 2.

4. Together write down some traditions that you would like to create for your family. What is the goal of each tradition and how are you going to accomplish it?

5. Pray about the memories that God would have you help create for your children.

6. Ask yourself, "What would I like for my children to be saying in twenty years about what they remember from their childhood?"

7. Jot down a few ideas about celebrating the following events. Then ask your mate to do the same. If your children are old enough, you may want to make it a family time.

This is how we would like to celebrate birthdays at our home:

_____

_____

_____

_____

_____

This is how we would like to celebrate Christmas at our home:

_____

_____

_____

_____

_____

This is how we would like to celebrate Easter at our home:

_____

_____

_____

_____

_____

This is how we would like to celebrate Thanksgiving at our home:

_____

_____

_____

_____

These are some fun family traditions that we would like to begin to develop for our family:

_____

_____

_____

_____

TEN

The Power of Prayer

I was teaching the children about confession and the peace that you feel when you have confronted a sin and confessed it. We talked about how 1 John 1:9 truly is a Christian's bar of soap. That night as we prayed as a family, Angela confessed. "Dear God, I am so sorry that I took Christopher's car and hid it in my panty drawer."

After prayer time Christopher flew out of the room and returned with his car. "So you took my car, huh?"

In complete innocence she responded, "How did you know?"

He promptly retorted, "I just heard you pray about it."

"I wasn't talking to you. I was talking to Jesus." Oh, that we may pray so directly to just You, Jesus. Teach us to pray as purely and innocently as a child.

❤ Preparation for Prayer

Once when I felt the older children at school (grades 6-9) were in a dry spell about prayer, I had a few fathers dress up as soldiers with pretend guns. In the middle of our prayer time, they burst into the room and yelled, "You're right, they are praying. Line them up. They're going to jail."

Needless to say this got their attention. We had studied about countries where people were not free to worship and pray, but I could tell the message had not hit home. From then on the children got more serious about their prayer life. It is a privilege to talk to our Heavenly Father.

In preparing children for a time of prayer, I tell them the only reason we close our eyes and fold our hands is because this helps us to focus more on God. If we're looking around or fidgeting with something, we are less likely to be focused on the Lord. Does God only answer prayers of children who sit quietly and close their eyes and fold their hands? No. God answers the prayers that we pray from our heart. But quiet hands help the heart to be more quiet.

Why do we pray in Jesus' name? Jesus is the road straight to God. When we pray, believing in the power of Jesus, our prayers are carried straight to the throne of heaven.

❤ *Patterns of Prayer*

One of the best patterns we have for prayer is "The Lord's Prayer," found in Matthew 6. I personally believe in starting to teach this prayer at the kindergarten level. Children *can* learn the words, but we must be careful to help them truly understand the words. Take time to go through the prayer phrase by phrase with your child. Help him to articulate it in his own words so when he prays it by rote, it will have a deeper impact on him.

For the most part, I discourage memorized prayers. They do expose children to prayer, at least on some level, and they do present a pattern of praying that may be helpful. However, memorized prayers do not teach a child how to pray sincerely from his own heart.

I think memorized prayers for children ages two or three are appropriate. This is the age they love to learn rhymes. When Angela was two, her Sunday School teacher taught her a memorized prayer to music. Regardless of where we were, when food was served, she broke into prayerful praise.

People who pray as well as non-prayers are encouraged when they see a two-year-old spontaneously break into prayer: "And a little child shall lead them...."

I believe we should also set a pattern of when we pray. I have tried to begin the day with the Lord, yet I continue to fail miserably in this area. I set the alarm, but I doze back for "five more minutes." When I do get to my prayer chair, I nod off. I have tried everything. This is embarrassing to state publicly.

I am a night person. I come alive about 9:00 each night and can easily stay up until 1:00 or 2:00 A.M. So my solution is to have my quiet time after everyone is asleep. I write in my journal, the children's journals, and finally my prayer journal. This process prepares my heart for a quiet, productive, and peaceful time with the Lord. I then read His Word, do my Bible study, and close with prayer time. This works well for me, but I still have the picture in my mind that the true Proverbs 31 woman would greet her Lord each day in prayer. So I continue to try to work into a regular morning time with God.

I discovered a wonderful little tract called, "Seven Minutes with God" (NavPress) that has helped give my weary body and mind focus in the morning. This is the structure:

One minute: Prepare Your Heart (Ps. 143:8).
Four minutes: Read Bible.
Two minutes: Prayer organized in the following ways:

A Adoration   1 Chronicles 29:11
C Confession   1 John 1:9
T Thanksgiving Ephesians 5:20
S Supplication Matthew 7:7

We also need to train our children to pray spontaneously, as the need comes up. When you are driving and see an ambulance or fire truck, pray or encourage the children to pray. Or pray for news events as you hear them on the radio.

♥ Praying Hand: Using Fingers to Teach Prayer

Here are some simple ways to help children learn to pray. As soon as your children want to pray spontaneously on their own, let them. But in the meantime, or if your children feel more secure with a pattern to follow, try these suggestions.

♥ Age Two

We fold our hands and as we wiggle our thumbs together, we pray, "Dear God."

As we wiggle our pointer fingers, we say, "Thank You for my family."

As we wiggle our middle fingers, we say, "Thank You for Jesus."

As we wiggle our ring fingers, we say, "Thank You for our church."

As we wiggle our baby fingers, we say, "In Jesus' name, Amen."

♥ Ages Three and Four

Thumbs: "I pray for my *family.*" (Thumbs are for those closest to us.)

Pointer fingers: "Thank You for my *friends.*"

Middle fingers: "Thank You for *Jesus* who died on the cross for my sins."

Ring fingers: "Thank You for the *Bible* and my *church.*"

Baby fingers: "Help me to be more like *Jesus.* In Jesus' name, Amen."

At age four children can add more specifics for each division. For example, I pray for Grandma's knee when I pray for my family.

♥ Age Five

Introduce the idea of **J**esus (thumbs)
> **O**thers (middle, pointer, ring fingers)
> **Y**ou (baby fingers)

Have them pray by first focusing on *Jesus*. They can thank Him, praise Him, or simply talk to Him. But their focus should be clearly on *Jesus*. Gently encourage children to focus on Jesus, not their wish list for Jesus.

Encourage statements that focus on Jesus	Discourage prayers that are still "I" oriented
"Thank You, Jesus, for loving me.	"Jesus, I want a new bike.
"Thank You, Jesus, for dying on the cross for my sins."	"Jesus, please help me pass this test."
"Thank You, Jesus, for helping me today."	*Please note: It's OK for a child to ask the Lord to help him. But at this time in our prayer growth we want to help the child get to know *Jesus*.
"Jesus, You are my best friend."	

Use the middle, pointer, and ring fingers to remind children to pray for *others*. We can help broaden the child's understanding of others to include neighbors, missionaries, teachers, the President, etc.

The *y* in Joy is for *you*. In this case it is your child. I say, "Now we have talked to *Jesus,* and prayed for *others,* now we can pray for *you*. What would *you* like to pray for, for *you*?"

The consistent pattern in all of these prayers is putting the child's needs last. Children at this age are in a very egocentric stage of development. We must gradually train in the Christlike attitude of putting others before us.

Here is one more reminder that we made up to stretch our

praying to a new level. The child goes through each of his ten fingers.

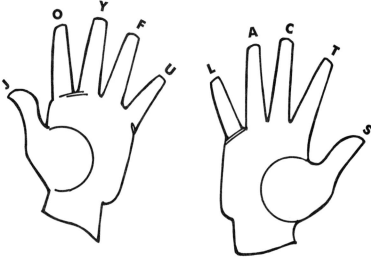

J esus
O thers
Y ou
F amily
U se me, Lord (Be willing to serve)
L oving (Even when it's hard)

A dore God (Praise)
C onfess specific sins
T hanksgiving
S upplication

These are simple little prayer reminders to help your child grow as a prayer warrior. You and your child can make up your own reminders. It's really a special time together.

❤ *Practical Projects*

We've tried different things to help us be more consistent in our prayer life. Perhaps one of these ideas will help you.

• *Prayer journals.* These are a nice way to keep up with

different things that you have prayed for as a family over the year.

● *Prayer power.* I made up this form and carry it with me everywhere in my time organizer.

Prayer Power

PRAISE

_____

_____

_____

CONFESSION

_____

_____

_____

THANKSGIVING

_____

_____

_____

FAMILY

Parents:

_____

_____

_____

"Mate-Date":

_____

_____

_____

THOSE IN THE MINISTRY:

Pastor(s): _____

_____

Teachers: _____

_____

Missionaries:

Local: _____

_____

Abroad: _____

_____

Board: _____

_____

THOSE IN GOVERNMENT:

National: _____

_____

State: _____

_____

Local: _____

_____

Issues: _____

_____

ME:

Spiritually: _____

_____

Children: Mentally: _____

_____   _____

_____   Emotionally: _____

_____   _____

                                My Relationships: _____
Extended Family:
                                _____
_____
                                Physically: _____
_____
                                _____
_____
                                My Work: _____
_____
                                _____
_____
                                My Attitudes: _____

_____   _____

- I put a *prayer column* on my daily "To Do" list.
- Each parent in our school has a child or two to pray for. I have their names on a 3x5 card, sitting on my desk. I write the specifics on the back where no one else can see them.
- In my "Family Files" (3x5 note card file box), I have tabs for:

  1. Daddy
  2. Mommy
  3. Damon
  4. Christopher
  5. Angela
  6. Family
  7. Church
  8. School
  9. Missions
  10. Answered Prayers!

As needs arise, I write them on a 3x5 card and file them in the box. At prayer time I distribute the cards to each family member so we take turns praying for the needs.

When we know the prayer is answered, we file the card away. You can start your own 3x5 card file box simply called "Answered Prayers" because you will run out of room in your other box. What a faith builder this box becomes. Be sure your children grow to understand that God's answer may be "no." It may not be the answer they wanted, but it is an answer. The "waits" are still in the first card file box. Only the clearly answered "yes" or "no" prayers are filed.

- *Prayer Trees.*
  1. Put the outline of a tree on a bulletin board by the kitchen table, your child's table, or some easy to reach place.
  2. Cut out shapes or items for your tree that change each month. For example:
     September: apples
     October: orange leaves
     November: tan leaves
     December: Christmas lights
     January: snowflakes
     February: hearts
     March: shamrocks
     April: lilies
     May: apple blossoms

These don't have to be authentic, botanical items. They can be a *symbol* to represent the holiday or month.

Either you or your child should write a prayer request and put it on the tree. Each day you should both look at the tree. When the request has been answered, the item moves to the bottom of the tree, on the ground. As the year advances, the top of the tree, as well as the ground under it becomes a kaleidoscope of prayer requests. Those on top are still unanswered and thus a visible reminder to keep on praying. Those on the bottom serve as a growing reminder of the many prayers God has answered. At the end of each year, gather up all the answered prayers, put them in a baggie, and place them in your children's memory boxes.

Please note, the year can begin whenever you want.

1. January to December (Calendar year)
2. September to August (School year)
3. On your child's birthday, so it will measure one year of his life.

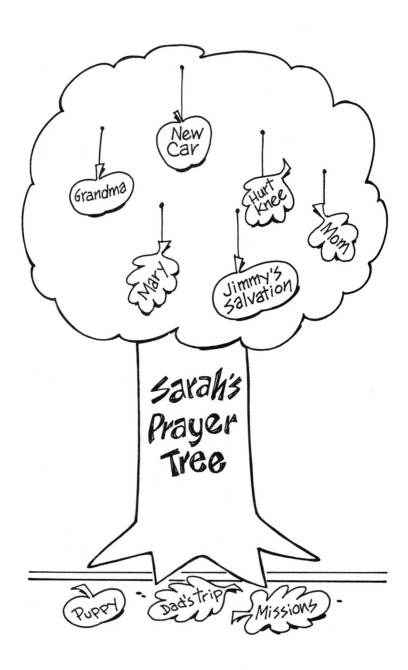

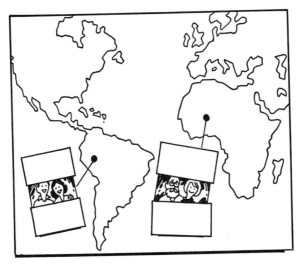

● *Missions Map.* On a world map, put a *picture* of a missionary that you pray for and then a 3x5 card of current prayer requests under it. Be sure the card can be easily changed. Have a child take a stick pin with yarn wrapped around it that goes from the picture to the place where they are serving. This activity provides:

　● a daily, visible reminder to pray for our missionaries.

　● a visual reminder that not all missionaries are in Africa. (Children often think all missionaries go to Africa.)

　● a sense of geography. When things happen in the news, you can look at the map to see where that place is.

♥ Praying for Fruit

Let us pray for our children to produce the fruit of the Spirit. One helpful way to do this is to select a key verse and pray that for our children.

♥ Love
I pray for my children to love as God loves.

　"Walk in love, just as Christ also loved you, and gave Himself up for us" (Eph. 5:2).

"Beloved, let us love one another, for love is from God; and everyone who loves is born of God and knows God" (1 John 4:7).

"God is love, and the one who abides in love abides in God, and God abides in him" (1 John 4:16).

"There is no fear in love; but perfect love casts out fear" (1 John 4:18).

❤ *Joy*

I pray for my children to experience the joy of the Lord when I pray this verse for them: "The joy of the Lord is your strength" (Neh. 8:10). I pray for them to know the joy that comes from

> Jesus
> Others
> You

❤ *Peace*

I pray for my children to know peace.

"And the peace of God which surpasses all comprehension, shall guard your hearts and minds in Christ Jesus" (Phil. 4:7).

"Peace I leave with you; My peace I give to you; not as the world gives, do I give to you. Let not your heart be troubled, nor let it be fearful" (John 14:27).

"Depart from evil, and do good; seek peace, and pursue it" (Ps. 34:14).

"Now may the Lord of peace Himself continually grant you peace in every circumstance. The Lord be with you all" (2 Thes. 3:16).

❤ *Patience*

I pray for my children to be patient in the power and strength of the Holy Spirit.

"You too be patient; strengthen your hearts" (James 5:8).

"Strengthened with all power, according to His glorious might, for the attaining of all steadfastness and patience; joyously" (Col. 1:11).

"Blessed is a man who perseveres under trial; for once he has been approved, he will receive the crown of life, which the Lord has promised to those who love Him" (James 1:12).

♥ *Kindness*

I pray for my children to be kind to one another in their speech and actions as they are filled with His loving-kindness.

"And be kind to one another, tenderhearted, forgiving each other, just as God in Christ also has forgiven you" (Eph. 4:32).

♥ *Goodness*

I pray for my children to exhibit the goodness that comes from a renewed spirit in Jesus Christ.

"To this end also we pray for you always that our God may count you worthy of your calling, and fulfill every desire for goodness and the work of faith with power" (2 Thes. 1:11).

"For we are His workmanship, created in Christ Jesus for good works, which God prepared beforehand, that we should walk in them" (Eph. 2:10).

♥ *Faithfulness*

First and foremost I pray for my children to come to faith in Jesus Christ as their Lord and Savior.

"For by grace you have been saved through faith; and that not of yourselves, it is the gift of God" (Eph. 2:8).

I pray my children's faith will grow strong in their daily walk with the Lord: "But I have prayed for you, that your faith may not fail; and you, when once you have turned again, strengthen your brothers" (Luke 22:32).

"Be on the alert, stand firm in the faith, act like men, be strong" (1 Cor. 16:13).

"Fight the good fight of faith" (1 Tim. 6:12).

I pray that my children will be ever faithful in service to the living God: "Therefore, since we receive a kingdom which cannot be shaken, let us show gratitude, by which we may offer to God an acceptable service with reverence and awe" (Heb. 12:28).

💜 Gentleness

I pray for my children to be "uncontentious, gentle, showing every consideration for all men" (Titus 3:2).

I also pray that they will "pursue righteousness, godliness, faith, love, perseverance, and gentleness" (1 Tim. 6:11).

I pray for my children to be the kind of people this verse describes so beautifully: "But let it be the hidden person of the heart, with the imperishable quality of a gentle and quiet spirit, which is precious in the sight of God" (1 Peter 3:4).

💜 Self-Control

I pray for my children to have the self-control that flows from a spirit-controlled life.

"But if you are led by the Spirit you are not under the law. . . . But the fruit of the Spirit is love, joy, peace, patience, kindness, goodness, faithfulness, gentleness, self-control; against such things there is no law. . . . If we live by the Spirit, let us also walk by the Spirit" (Gal. 5:18, 22-23, 25).

💜 **Pray without Ceasing**

I wanted the children at school and church to realize that prayer was not confined to a particular place, time, or physical position such as hands folded/eyes closed. I used 1 Thessalonians 5:17 as the Scripture to encourage them to pray (talk to God) anytime, anywhere and for any reason. I also wanted them to realize that God may talk to us anytime, anywhere, and for any reason. We may be riding our bikes when we hear the Lord calling us to do something. Does He yell? No. It's a still, quiet voice. Does He only call us for the "big jobs" like being a missionary in Africa, or can He call us for the seemingly "little jobs" as well such as helping our neighbor carry in groceries?

My goal was to help train the children to "practice the

presence" of God as a daily habit. I wanted them to talk to their Heavenly Father about all their needs and be attuned to listen to His still, quiet voice and respond with obedience. Thus, I reminded them to "pray without ceasing."

One day as the children were leaving chapel and I was collecting hugs at the door, one little guy said, "I'm sorry I sneezed during your prayer, Mrs. Capehart." I hugged him and assured him that it was no problem because we certainly can't control when those 'ole sneezes come. He responded, "But I know you like us to pray without sneezing." Isn't that wonderful? So, you may pray and sneeze, but please don't cease praying. May God bless you as you grow in your own prayer life by praying with and for your child.

❤ Parent Participation

1. What do you pray for your children?
2. Take a 3x5 note card and jot down three things that you want to pray for your child this week.
3. Look back after a few weeks and make a note of answers to prayers.
4. Pray with your child this week. If this is a new experience for you, pray the Lord's prayer with your child. Slowly begin to pray about other matters with your child.
5. What fruits of the Spirit would you like to pray for your child this week? Find a key verse for each of the fruits of the Spirit to pray for your child.

Love:
Prayer Request:

Verse:

Joy:
Prayer Request:

Verse:

Peace:
Prayer Request:

Verse:

Patience:
Prayer Request:

Verse:

Kindness:
Prayer Request:

Verse:

Goodness:
Prayer Request:

Verse:

Faithfulness:
Prayer Request:

Verse:

Gentleness:
Prayer Request:

Verse:

Self-Control:
Prayer Request:

Verse:

ELEVEN

Walking Your Talk

I had just returned from a pastor's planning retreat. My church desk was covered with pink phone messages. I gathered them up, put them in my organizer with the hope of returning a few of the most urgent. I did car pool, then took my children to a Christian school where I was scheduled to do teacher training. The children and I had lots to catch up on and did so in the car. In the process of unloading to do the seminar, my shoulder became disengaged, and I was in excruciating pain in addition to losing the use of the upper left part of my body. I took pain medication and managed to get through the seminar. I got home late and tried to make plans to get in to see my doctor even though it was past hours.

Then I realized that one of my children had taken something from the school where I had just done the seminar. I questioned him. First denial, then confession. We decided that the "consequence" was that he must go in and talk to the principal of the other school right after school the next day. We shed tears and finally, after a two hour discussion, some maturing Christlike behavior emerged.

That night was a major turning point for him. It was one of those perfect "teachable" moments. But, not at the "perfect" time for Mom. By evening my pain had become unbearable. No chance of getting to my doctor. My daughter was now crying in her room. "Why does he get to have you all alone? I missed you too." I went to spend time with her.

Knock, knock. Enter teenage son: "Mom, there are eight messages for you since 7:00 tonight. Two say they have to talk to you tonight. By the way, I'm waiting on you to help me with my homework."

My pity party parade escalated as I realized that tomorrow was the one day I had to write the final chapter of this book. How could I write in this pain? With all the calls to return? Teachers to recruit? House to clean? Special dinner to prepare?

I began to pray fervently. I called my dear friend and prayer warrior. OK, she was praying. I was back on duty.

The children and I all prayed together. Then we had books and snuggles for little ones, got the oldest one going on homework, and focused on the middle one who was still working through the crisis. *God's grace is sufficient, He won't give more than I am able to bear.*

Words suddenly broke the barrier of my inner dialogue:

"Mom, you really helped me tonight. Thanks for talking to me all this time. I really understand that what I did was wrong. I'm ready to apologize to the principal. I love you, Mom. Sweet dreams. Oh, Mom, could we pray one more time? I want to tell God thanks for helping me grow as a Christian tonight."

Amen. Amen. Amen. In tears I collapsed on my bed. No longer tears of pity and pain, but tears of joy. *Thank You, Lord, for giving me Your grace so that I could give to my child. Was this Your divine preparation course so that I could write this chapter? No pain, no gain, huh? You're really going to make me walk my talk, aren't You?*

While waiting for my husband to return from work to put my shoulder back in place so I could sleep, I reflected upon what it really means to "walk your talk."

Before this experience, I had been planning to structure this chapter around the idea of consistency between our talk and our walk. In other words, wanting our children to see that we are trying to live out the words we say to them about our convictions. But now I could see the Lord adding a new dimension to this idea of walking our talk: letting our children see us turn to Christ when we are under tremendous pressure. God set up the particulars of my situation that night for His divine purpose. I believe that my son grew more because of my own personal situation. He knows that when I am in this level of physical pain, I can barely function. It would have been easy for me to say that we would deal with the problem at another time. But for him, it was the perfect teachable moment. He had to know on some level that I was making a commitment to him and his struggle and that it was truly the Lord who was granting me the grace to continue. In my weakness, Christ could become more evident.

❤ *Walking Our Talk Under Stress*

I am well aware that I am at my worst when I am in a hurry. I once heard that hurry is not *of* the devil, it *is* the devil! That's true for me. I am *not* at my best when I'm in a hurry. I'm impatient. I do not always "practice what I preach."

Reality dictates that on Saturday nights I often rush in from speaking somewhere, feed everyone, drop the oldest at his function, take the two youngest, and rush to church to prepare everything for Sunday. The race continues. We rush home and while they shower, I do the dishes, throw in the laundry, and climb on the bed for a time of prayer together. This is the reality of life at this season. If I complain because it's not the way I want it to be, my children feel it. If I make it a funny game, they love it. I often hold the power of their perceptions of how life can be on a Saturday night. I guard that responsibility. I pray for God's grace so my children see *joy* in my walk and talk.

A parent of a former student had a party for all the kids who were now in high school and no longer at our school. I couldn't attend because I was out of town. She told me the kids were all sharing memories. She said she was touched by their favorite memory of me: "No matter how tough things got she always smiled and always loved us and made us feel that she was happy to be there." Their favorite specific memory was not one I would have ever guessed. I would have preferred it be a moment from chapel or a Bible lesson. But no, it was a time that I was under the most stress ever. I remember it as a time that I was barely hanging on. They remembered me as "smiling and being loving when most people would have walked away."

I remember feeling like a failure at that time. I was dumbfounded as I heard this. I do not share this story to brag; I share it as one of those reference points that I keep looking back to. Why then? I was a mess. Why don't they remember when I had a good chapel lesson planned? Why? Because children study *character*. They watch us. They study us. They learn far more from what we *are* than what we do or say. They look for Jesus in us.

When I thought I was in perfect control, they didn't notice. When I knew I was a wreck and the Lord was carrying me, they saw *His* Spirit come through. I can, in all humility, go back to those kids and say, "That wasn't me, kids; what you saw was the Lord."

💜 Talking Our Walk

Just as we need to "walk our talk," we also need to "talk our walk." By this I mean we need to take time to discuss what our walk as a Christian is all about with our children.

The market today is saturated with children's books on the Word. There are Bible story books as well as Christian character books. It is an amazing dichotomy that at a time of such abundance in spiritual communication, we live in a world of escalating evil. We cannot protect our children from the world; its influence is ever-present. Billboards, television, movies, and obscene literature scream out the messages of sex, corruption, and sin.

As parents, we want to protect our children from evil. We may decide to put them in a Christian school or to teach them at home. We may enroll them in Christian clubs or civic organizations that promote "good" character. We may choose to read them only Christian literature, allow them to listen to only Christian radio, and tightly screen or omit television programs or movies. You ask, what else can I do?

Talk your walk with your children. This is one of the best ways to bond your children to the Christian worldview. Of course, you should still pray together, read the Word, and enjoy family devotions. But when we go beyond the "shoulds, oughts, and pat answers" to truly talking and carefully communicating our convictions, something happens. There is nothing richer than soul to soul communication. Children sense when our words have the authenticity of experience.

This does not mean we have all the answers. But it does mean we have the sincerity to state our sins, the courage to communicate our convictions, and the resolve to repent from our old ways. Children always respect truth.

When we are open and receptive to the leading of the Holy Spirit and we share what we are learning with transparency, our children respond. It is a bond of steel. Talk with your children about the blood of Jesus, the power that Satan has on this earth, the insidiousness of sin, and the trap of temptation.

♥ *Teaching Biblical Truths for Application*

I believe children can become "Bible smart" very quickly; however, we don't often stretch them further into the wisdom of application.

I find that when I teach a lesson from the Bible on the factual level, I get a factual response. Yes, Noah built an ark. Yes, he took the animals two by two. Yes, it rained for forty days. True, true. But are those facts life-changing? Will that knowledge help a child live in a corrupt world full of diminishing values? Probably not.

We must send our children out into the world with convictions of steel. These come only from:

- Salvation
- Bible Teaching
- Prayer
- Application

Application comes only when the child sees the relevancy of the Bible truth to his life today. Your child will probably not be asked to build an ark. He will most likely not be swallowed and transported to obedience via the whale express. So when teaching these biblical stories, it is critical to go beyond the factual level of understanding. Learning the facts of a Bible story is a peripheral experience. It is when the child sees the underlying message and how it lives out, then the transformation of character emerges.

We must help them see how incredibly amazing it was that Noah did build the ark. We see cute Noah's Ark pictures everywhere. We think it's a sweet story. We need to teach it as the profound reality of a man who trusted in God with perfect obedience. Children need to realize that Noah built an ark bigger than many of our churches. He built it with no architect or modern machinery. He built it step-by-step in submission to the Lord's leading. There was no waterway to float this boat. People were laughing at him. He did appear "crazy" in the eyes of the world. But Noah was a man of God, committed to walking in obedience. This is the level of commitment to God we want our children to have.

Children love to hear about David and Goliath. They love to role play David killing Goliath. But what about the David who loved the sheep, foreshadowing a Savior who would love His lambs? What about the David who fell into sin and was broken and contrite before God? Children need to see that God loved David "as a man after God's own heart." God loved David's transparency and yielded spirit. Through the life of David, God shows how He loves even the sinner. In that love He can use us, even with our sin. But we must still suffer the consequences of our sin. Children need to see how

God works not only in the lives of Bible characters, but also in our lives today. Children need to be given a window into how David felt, why Noah obeyed, why Moses doubted himself, and how Adam rationalized his sin. If children don't see the relevancy to their lives today, then they will set their Bibles back on the shelf as a simple reference book and not as *the* guidebook of holy living today.

Parents, walk your talk so children can see a consistent life of faithfulness. Talk your walk so children hear of a life transformed by a living Savior. Walk and talk your children through the mountains and valleys of your life so they can experience, however vicariously, how God works in your life. Show your children how to live Christlike character in the most trying of circumstances. Model prayer as the place where we fuel up to fight the enemy and the Word as the source of that fuel.

My dear freind Sue Bohlin had polio as a child. She often dreamed of being a beautiful princess and being able to run and play as other children did. She resented deeply the bondage of her polio. When she became a Christan, she truly believed that God would perform a miracle and heal her. Each night she prayed with all the gusto she could, sure that the next morning she would get up and waltz out of bed. She would use this healing as a powerful testimony to tell others about the greatness of our God. But each morning she awakened to the pain of her polio. She was becoming a bitter, disillusioned Christian. One day, when she was remembering her old fantasy of being a princess, the Lord gently reminded her that, as a Christian, she was a child of a King. She quickly responded with, "If I am a child of a King, then I *AM A PRINCESS!*" If you knew Sue now, you would realize that she is indeed a princess and that even in the bondage of her polio, she is free in Jesus Christ. That can be a far more powerful testimony than being healed of polio. Paul said, "In my weakness, Thou are made great." Sue lives those words.

When we look at a tapestry we often see a pretty picture or design, but if we were to turn it over we would see loose threads that are anything but pretty. I believe that we often see life from the back of the tapestry and the threads seem loose and without pattern or beauty. But when we, like Sue Bohlin, get a glimpse of the other side, from God's point of view, we feel His deep abiding peace, joy, and gentleness. Then we are able to "walk our talk" in the midst of daily challenges and problems, and we have helped our children know what is truly valuable in life.

❤ *Parent Participation*

1. Have you ever told your children how you became a Christian? They would love to hear it.

2. Have you ever told your children what you were like before you became a Christian? They'll love this.

3. Tell your children about a time when you wavered in your walk and how the Lord got you back on track.

4. Be willing to share your personal failures in a transparent way.

5. Share times of transformation and renewing of spirit. Children love to hear your successes also.

6. Be a model of a prayer warrior. Let your children see you turn to the Living Word and the power of prayer to equip you to lead a godly life.

7. True repentance means turning from sin and turning to Jesus Christ. That is the message of the Gospel. What is the Gospel message your children are getting from you?

Suggested Reading

Chapter One

Ilg, M.D., Frances L., et al. *Child Behavior.* New York: Barnes and Noble Books, A Division of Harper and Row, 1981.

LaHaye, Dr. Tim. *Transformed Temperaments.* Wheaton, Illinois: Tyndale House Publishers, 1971.

Littauer, Florence. *Raising the Curtain on Raising Children.* Waco, Texas: Word Publisher, 1988.

Meier, Paul. *Christian Child Rearing and Personality Development.* Grand Rapids: Baker Book House, 1977.

Neff, LaVonne. *One of a Kind.* Portland: Multnomah Press, 1988.

White, Burton L. *The First Three Years of Life.* Prentice-Hall, Inc., 1975.

Chapter Two

Fuller, Cheri. *Home Life.* Tulsa, Oklahoma: Honor Books, 1988.

Hendricks, Howard. *Heaven Help the Home.* Wheaton: Victor Books, 1982.

Kohlenberger, Carolyn and Noel Wescombe. *Raising Wise Children—How To Teach Your Child To Think.* Portland: Multnomah Press, 1990.

McEwan, Elaine K. *Super Kid? Raising Balanced Kids in a Super Kid World.* Elgin, Illinois: David C. Cook Publishing Co., 1988.

Zacharias, Raye. *Styles and Profiles.* 1217 Whispering Lane, South Lake, Texas 76092.

Chapter Three

Caplan, Frank and Teresa. *The Power of Play.* 1973.

Elkind, David. *The Hurried Child.* Reading, Mass.: Addison-Wesley Publishing Company, 1981.

Montessori, Maria. *The Absorbent Mind.* New York: A Delta Book, Dell Publishing Company, 1967.

Piers, Maria W. and Genevieve Millet Landau. *The Gift of Play.* New York: Walker and Company, 1980.

Standing, E.M. *The Montessori Revolution.* New York: Schocken Books, 1962.

Chapter Four

Ames, Dr. Louise Bates. *He Hit Me First.* New York: Dember Books, 1982.

Dobson, Dr. James. *Dare to Discipline.* Waco, Texas: Word Books, 1987.

Dobson, Dr. James. *Parenting Isn't for Cowards.* Waco, Texas: Word Books, 1987.

Dobson, Dr. James. *The Strong-Willed Child.* Wheaton, Illinois: Tyndale House Publishers, 1982.

Leman, Dr. Kevin. *Making Children Mind Without Losing Yours.* Old Tappan, New Jersey: Fleming H. Revell Company, 1984.

Chapter Five

Arndt, Elise. *A Mother's Touch.* Wheaton, Illinois: Victor Books, 1987.

Campbell, Dr. Ross. *How to Really Love Your Child.* Wheaton, Illinois: Victor Books, 1987.

Chapter Six

Briggs, Dorothy. *Your Child's Self-Esteem: The Key to His Life.* Garden City, New York: Doubleday, 1970.

Dobson, Dr. James. *Hide or Seek.* Old Tappan, New Jersey: Fleming Revell, 1974.

Chapter Seven

Cline, M.D., Foster and Jim Fay. *Parenting With Love and Logic.* Colorado Springs, Colorado: NavPress, 1980.

Phillips, Mike. *Building Respect, Responsibility and Spiritual Values in Your Child.* Minneapolis: Bethany House Publishers, 1981.

Chapter Eight

Arndt, Elise. *A Mother's Time.* Wheaton, Illinois: Victor Books, 1989.

Barnes, Emily. *More Hours in My Day.* Eugene, Oregon: Harvest House Publishers, 1984.

Hunt, Gladys. *Honey for a Child's Heart.* Grand Rapids: Zondervan, 1969.

Nahmer, Nancy L. *A Parent's Guide to Christian Books for Children.* Wheaton, Illinois: Tyndale House Publishers, 1984.

Trelease, Jim. *The Read Aloud Handbook.* Penguin Books, 1979.

Wilson, Elizabeth. *Books Children Love.* Crossway Books, 1987.

Chapter Nine

Birkey, Verna and Jeanette Turnquist. *Building Happy Memories and Family Traditions.* Old Tappan, New Jersey: Fleming H. Revell Company, 1980.

Gaither, Gloria and Shirley Dobson. *Let's Make a Memory.* Waco, Texas: Word Books, 1983.

Hibbard, Ann. *Family Celebrations.* Brentwood, Tennessee: Wolgemuth and Hyatt Publishing, 1988.

Child Evangelism Fellowship, check local areas.

To order personalized books and tapes contact Terrie's Tapes, 1109 Quail Hollow, Garland, Texas, 75043.

Chapter Ten

Beers, Gilbert V. *Parents, Talk With Your Children.* Eugene, Oregon: Harvest House, 1988.

Chapin, Alice. *Building Your Child's Faith.* Nashville, Tennessee: Thomas Nelson Publishers, 1990.

Chapter Eleven

Haystead, Wes. *Teaching Your Child about God.* Ventura, California: Regal Books, Div. of GL, 1981.

Other Books:

Christenson, Evelyn. *What Happens When Women Pray* and *Lord Change Me.* Wheaton, Illinois: Victor Books, 1975.

Christenson, Larry. *The Christian Family.* Minneapolis: Bethany House Publishers, 1974.

Dickinson, Richard W. and Carole Gift Page. *The Child In Each of Us.* Wheaton, Illinois: Victor Books, 1989.

Dobson, Dr. James. *Love Must Be Tough*. Waco, Texas: Word Books, 1986.

Hansel, Tim. *What Kids Need Most in a Dad*. Old Tappan, New Jersey: Fleming H. Revell, 1984.

Ketterman, M.D. Grace. *You and Your Child's Problems*. Old Tappan, New Jersey: Fleming H. Revell, 1983.

Kidder, Virelle. *Mothering Upstream*. Wheaton, Illinois: Victor, 1990.

Kimmel, Tim. *Legacy of Love: A Plan for Parenting on Purpose*. Portland: Multnomah Press, 1989.

Lush, Jean with Pamela Vredevelt. *Mothers and Sons*. Old Tappan, New Jersey: Fleming H. Revell, 1988.

Meier, Paul. *Christian Child Rearing and Personality Development*. Grand Rapids, Baker Book House, 1977.

Money, Royce. *Building Stronger Families*. Wheaton, Illinois: 1988.

Narramore, Bruce. *Why Children Misbehave*. Grand Rapids: Zondervan, 1980.

Ortlund, Anne. *Children Are Wet Cement*. Old Tappan, New Jersey: Fleming H. Revell, 1981.

Parents and Children. Jay Kesler, et. al., Editors. Wheaton, Illinois: Victor Books, 1986.

Rogers, Fred. *Mister Rogers Talks with Parents*. New York: Berkley Books, 1983.

Schaeffer, Edith. *What Is a Family?* Old Tappan, New Jersey: Fleming H. Revell, 1975.

Smalley, Gary. *The Key to Your Child's Heart*. Waco, Texas: Word Books, 1984.

Stanley, Charles. *How To Keep Your Kids on Your Team*. Nashville, Tennessee: Thomas Nelson Publishers, 1985.

Swindoll, Charles. *Growing Wise in Family Life.* Portland: Multnomah Press, 1988.

Ziglar, Zig. *Raising Positive Kids in a Negative World.* Nashville, Tennessee: Thomas Nelson Publishers, 1985.